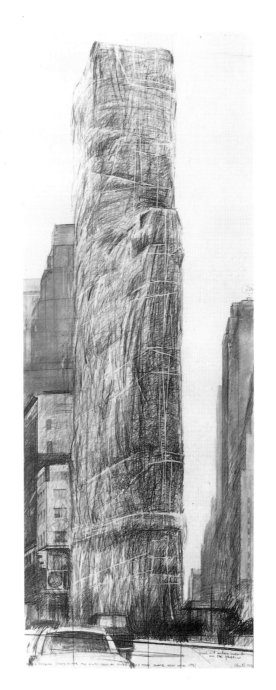

Christo

Jeanne-Claude

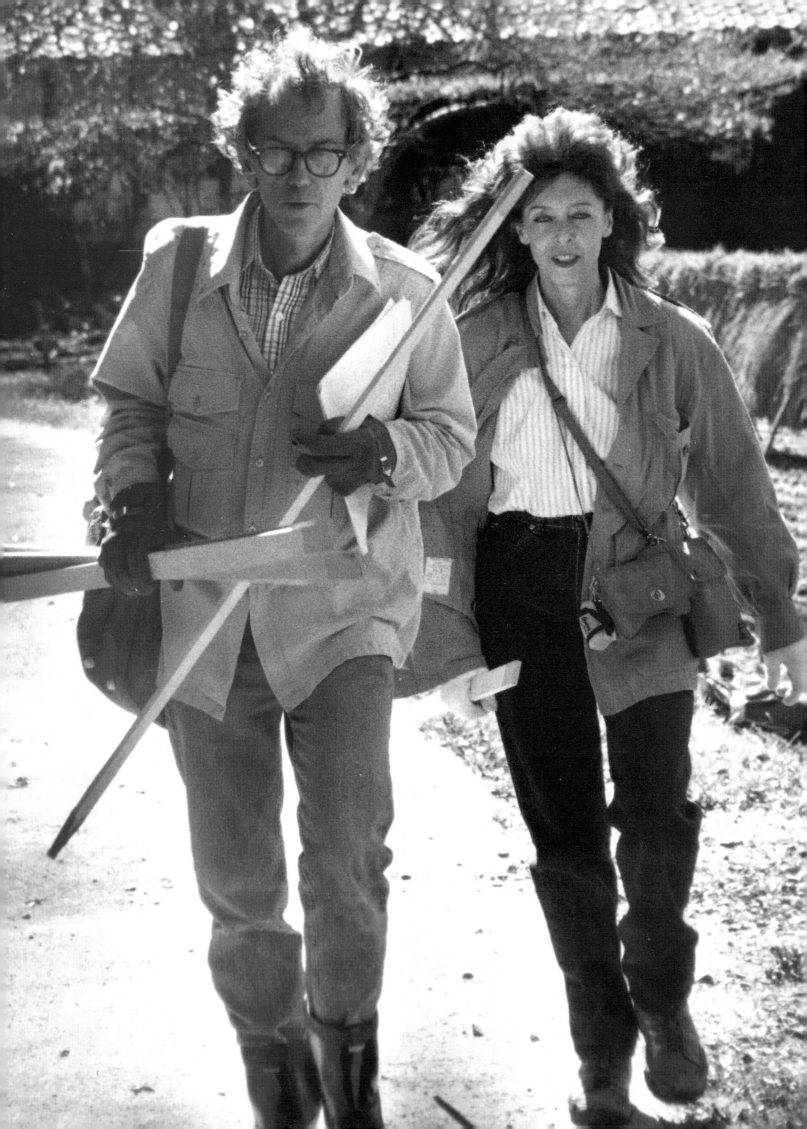

Jacob Baal-Teshuva

CHRISTO
&
JEANNE-CLAUDE

Photographs by
Wolfgang Volz

Benedikt Taschen

To my wife Aviva with love
Jacob Baal-Teshuva

**This book was printed on 100% chlorine-free bleached
paper in accordance with the TCF standard.**

Original edition
© 1995 Benedikt Taschen Verlag GmbH
Hohenzollernring 53, D-50672 Köln
© 1995 Christo, New York
© 1995 VG Bild-Kunst, Bonn, for the work by Man Ray
© 1995 The Henry Moore Foundation, Hartfordshire, for the work by Henry Moore

Edited by Simone Philippi and Charles Brace, Cologne
Design: Simone Philippi, Cologne
Cover Design: Angelika Muthesius, Cologne

Printed in Germany
ISBN 3-8228-8884-2
GB

Contents

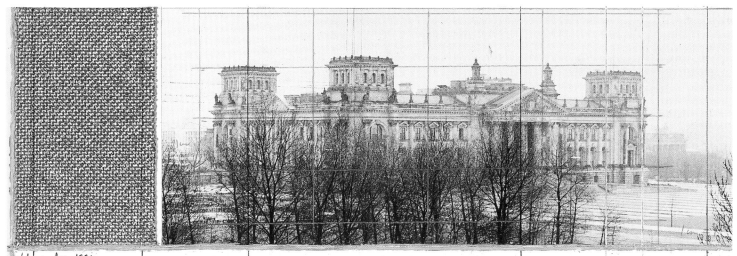

Christo 1994
WRAPPED REICHSTAG (PROJECT FOR BERLIN) PLATZ DER REPUBLIK, SCHEIDEMANNSTR. BRANDENBURGER TOR, SPREE

height 42.5 meter (west portal 39.00 meter)   135.76 meter   96.00 M. (south portal 20.00 m)
tower height 6.00 meter

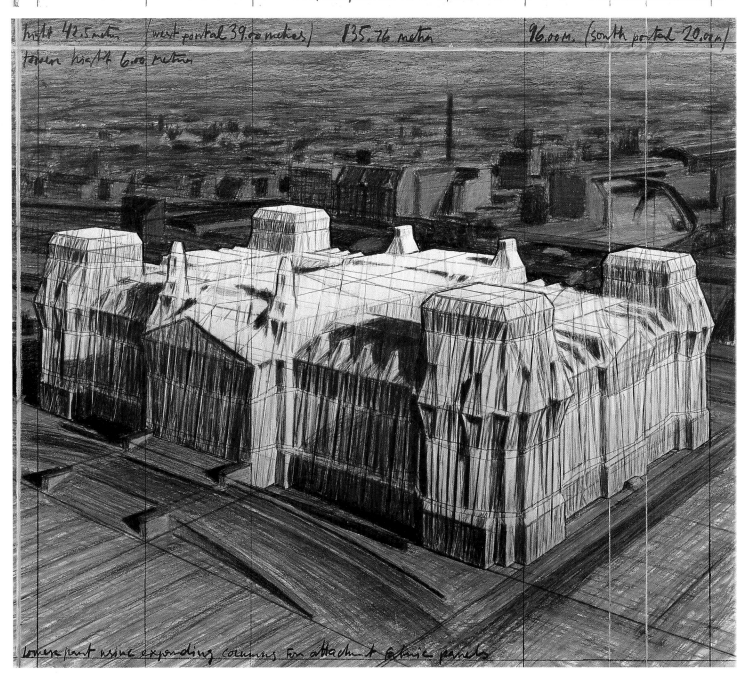

lower part using expanding columns for attachment fabric panels

After 23 years: "We have won"

The Reichstag triumph

On 25 February 1994 I was woken at six in the morning by the fax. The message, from Christo's indefatigable collaborator and partner Jeanne-Claude, was one I had long been waiting for: "WE HAVE WON. Permission was given to create the temporary work of art *Wrapped Reichstag, Project for Berlin*. The vote was 292 in favor, 223 against, with 9 abstentions."

The vote had been won in the German Bundestag in Bonn against all odds. Christo himself had sat in the visitors' gallery with his exclusive photographer Wolfgang Volz and Volz's wife Sylvia, following the final emotional debate with the help of an interpreter, and witnessing the triumphant outcome of twenty-three years of campaigning. The project, felt Christo, had become more important than ever in the period since German reunification, with the Reichstag set to become the seat of the German Parliament again. Jubilant, he told *The New York Times* that the vote in his favor was "a demonstration of the power, magnitude and fortitude of the project".

But the road to victory had been a controversial one. The Reichstag, built for the fledgling empire of Kaiser Wilhelm II in the 1890s, is a potent symbol of both the good and bad in German history. The republic of 1918 was proclaimed from the Reichstag; the fire in the building provided newly appointed Chancellor Adolf Hitler with an excuse for Communist-baiting and crack-downs in 1933; and the Red Army soldier who raised the hammer-and-sickle flag on the Reichstag in 1945 eloquently drove the last nail into the coffin of the 1,000-year Nazi Reich. Opponents of the Christos' project, especially in Chancellor Helmut Kohl's Christian Democratic Union (but also including prominent leftists such as writer Günter Grass), saw the proposed wrapping as a violation of the dignity of Germany's most powerful historic symbol. If the Christos proposed to wrap the Capitol in Washington or the Palace of Westminster, one FDP Bundestag member pointed out, there would be an outcry. Chancellor Kohl was adamant throughout in his opposition to the artists who said they wanted to do with the Reichstag what Picasso did with *Guernica*. Kohl's closest ally, Wolfgang Schäuble, leader of the parliamentary CDU, speaking in the Bundestag debate, stated the case against the project in carefully considered terms: "I have great respect for Christo's works and achievements. His art seems to me to have great esthetic value, and it teaches us to see things in new ways. I have been impressed by his works, such as the islands in Florida that he surrounded with pink fabric, the umbrellas landscapes he erected in Japan and California, the giant fence he built across California, and most recently his wrapping of the Pont-Neuf in Paris. These are experiments. We need not avoid all experimentation, but because of what the Reichstag represents, it should not be the subject of experimentation. The Reichstag is a major political symbol, a symbol that like no other represents the heights and depths of our history. Symbols of

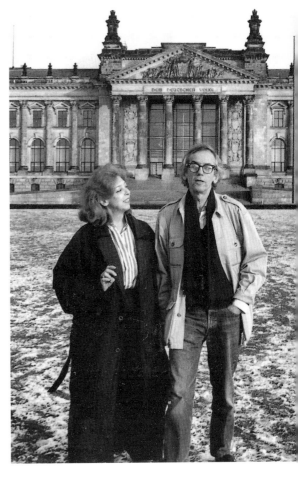

Jeanne-Claude and Christo in front of the Reichstag in Berlin, 1993

PAGE 6:
Wrapped Reichstag, Project for Berlin
Collage, 1994 in two parts
Pencil, fabric, twine, pastel, charcoal, photograph by Wolfgang Volz, crayon and fabric sample, 30.5 x 77.5 cm and 66.7 x 77.5 cm
New York, Collection Jeanne-Claude Christo

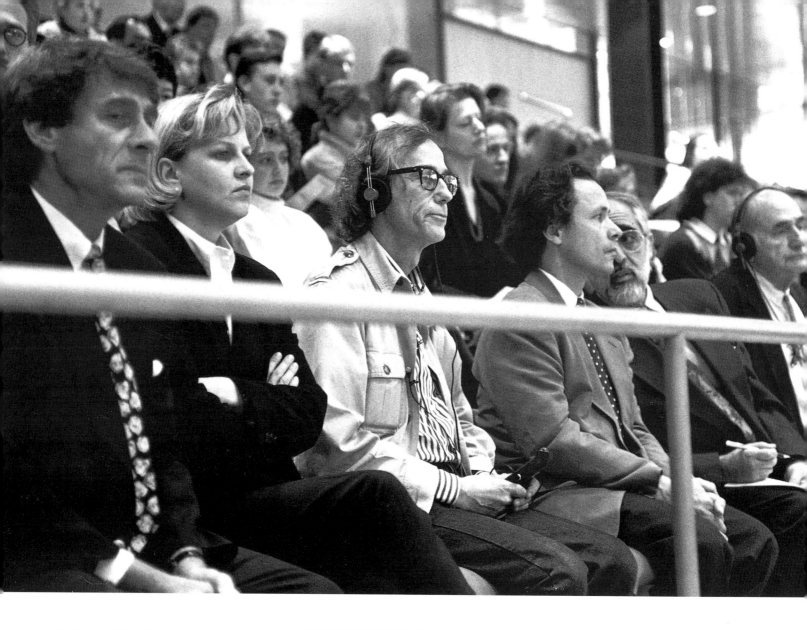

During the full parliamentary session at the Bonn Bundestag, February 25, 1994. From left to right: Roland Specker, project manager; Sylvia Volz; Christo; Wolfgang Volz, project manager; Michael Cullen, project historian and Thomas Golden.

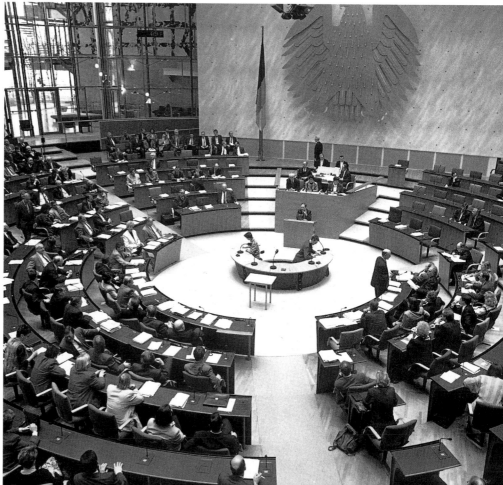

During the full parliamentary session at the Bonn Bundestag, 1994

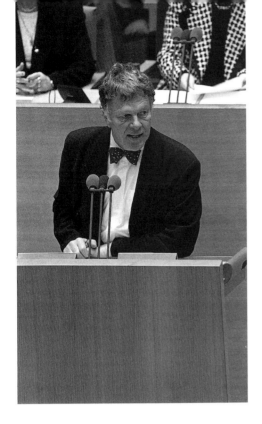

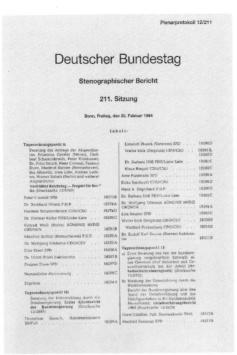

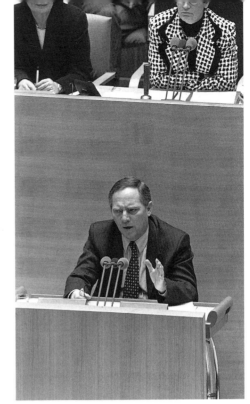

state, and all symbols, should bring people together. Wrapping the Reichstag would not unite, it would polarize."

Those who took the Christos' part felt that to reject their project would not only bar artistic freedom but also entrench political life in taboos. "By wrapping this building," Bundestag President Rita Süssmuth observed (*The New York Times*, January 7, 1993), "the artist not only displays his own feelings, but also gives citizens a chance to react to an edifice that is so important both to their tradition and their future." Süssmuth, a staunch supporter of the project for many years despite her CDU alignment, was not alone in urging its importance. It was widely understood that a more light-hearted Germany, a Germany emancipated from nationalism and narrow-mindedness, would be showcased by the Reichstag wrapping. In the debate, the main speech in favor was given by Social Democrat Peter Conradi: "This wrapping will insult neither the Reichstag building nor German history, and will be a wonderful cultural symbol of our new beginning in Berlin. Like a prized gift, the Reichstag will become more valuable, not less valuable, after it is beautifully wrapped. With this act, we want to give a positive sign, a beautiful, illuminating signal that fosters hope, courage and self-confidence." And Berlin's mayor, Eberhard Diepgen, doubtless sharing the feelings of many who were disappointed that the city failed in its bid to host the 2000 Olympics, rejoiced once the Bundestag vote had gone in favor: "Once more the eyes of the world will be on Berlin."

Helmut Kohl, who (the Christos reported) never answered the artists' letters requesting a meeting, was presumably less than enthusiastic at the result of the vote. And the eminent historian Nicolaus Sombart was quoted in *The Art Journal* (April 1994) as feeling the right time had passed: "it would be better to abandon the project". Other intellectuals were ironic: Berlin publisher Klaus Wagenbach wryly remarked that it would have been better to wrap the wall while it still stood (The Christos had in fact once planned a Berlin wall project similar in nature to their later *Running Fence* (p.51), and writer Irene Dische commented: "Personally, I would have preferred to see the Minister of the Interior and a few other politicians wrapped up so that we wouldn't have to hear from them for several weeks."

LEFT:
Member of the German Bundestag Peter Conradi (SPD) during his speech in favor of the *Wrapped Reichstag*, 1994

CENTRE:
Cover page of the transcript of the debate and vote of session number 211 of the German Parliament, 1994

RIGHT:
During an 18-minute speech, Wolfgang Schäuble (CDU) tried to rally his party against the *Wrapped Reichstag*, 1994

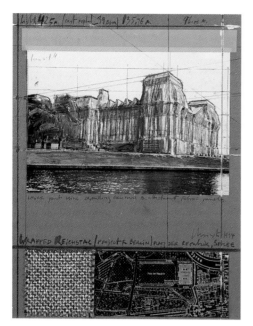

Wrapped Reichstag, Project for Berlin
Collage, 1994
Pencil, enamel paint, charcoal, crayon, ball-
point pen, map, photograph by Wolfgang
Volz, tape and fabric sample on brown/grey
cardboard, 35.5 x 28 cm
New York, Collection Adrian Keller

But there were many who shared the jubilation of Christo and Jeanne-
Claude. Film director Volker Schlöndorff felt that "any project that turns the
spotlights on the city, awakens interest and draws attention from both Ger-
mans and other Europeans, is welcome".

The Christos immediately returned to the mammoth-scale planning
involved in the project – scheduled to take place on June 17, 1995, weather
permitting, and to be completed by June 23 – together with their core team of
Wolfgang and Sylvia Volz and Roland Specker (the project's managers and
chief executive officers), and Michael S. Cullen (project historian), whose
idea the wrapping of the Reichstag had originally been, as we shall see later.

At the time of writing, the Reichstag wrapping – which will be financed
entirely from the sale of Christo's drawings, collages, scale models and early
work, to the tune of $5 to 7 million – still lies in the future. But the energy,
commitment and imaginative force of Christo and Jeanne-Claude is already
a fact of historical record; nobody doubts that they will achieve what they
have set out to achieve.

Interviewed by Michael Farr for the magazine *Modern Painters*, Christo
described the thick fabric he plans to use for the wrapping: "It will create
very rich angular folds, almost Gothic, incredibly beautiful. In June 1993 we
unfurled that fabric and photographed it on a rainy day, on a grey day to see
how the fabric looked, then with the light, the sun: we loved that sample. It
is very translucent fabric… it is not painted silver, but actually real aluminum powder is electrified on the surface."

Christo has given careful thought to the nature of form and transformation. "Today the Reichstag is very full of details, very broken, all these little
ornaments and fragments, and when it will be wrapped only the fabric will
really create a new form.

"There will be only the fabric to give a completely new form – the folds
of silver fabric cascading from the top like a waterfall, highlighting the
many points that cannot be seen today in the real architecture. The fabric
will be off the wall – 1 or 2 meters off – allowing the cloth to breathe and to
give this constant motion unlike the normal architecture of very sturdy materials; the material will be always moving with the wind."

The Christos' projects are always meticulously planned. "The wrapping
will be a very fast operation. First in the factory, off site. Making the fabric,
sewing it, folding the sections, prefabricating special cages of steel to pro-
tect the ornaments. We will bring all this hardware up there; first we will
condition the roof of the building to become like a working platform – with
wood, plywood and special steel parts. We would like to do the actual wrapping starting on Saturday and finishing in four or five days – probably using
200 iron workers."

Following the long controversies that preceded the Bundestag vote, the
Christos know they can expect a mixed reception to the Reichstag wrapping;
but Jeanne-Claude puts their feelings with stylish irony when she says the
wrapping will make "100 per cent of the people of Germany happy because
whatever percentage – let's imagine 80 per cent – will be happy because
they have seen the wrapped Reichstag, the 20 per cent who were furious
about it will be so happy when we unwrap it!"

Christo and Jeanne-Claude, a formidable team for over three decades,
are well matched in their tenacity and appetite for hard work, and Jeanne-
Claude's organizational skills (she is a general's daughter) match the drive
and creative genius of her husband. For both, inspiration is a very personal
matter. A project may originate in a memory, a smell, in an elusive attachment to a place, or in many other things; but at the end of the complex logist-

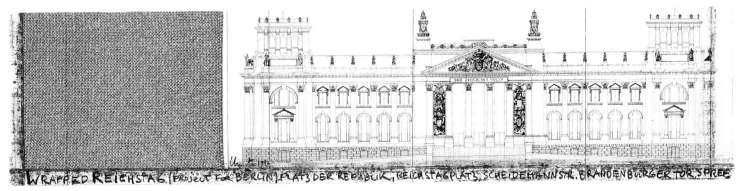

WRAPPED REICHSTAG. (PROJECT FOR BERLIN) PLATZ DER REPUBLIK, REICHSTAGPLATS, SCHEIDEMANNSTR, BRANDENBURGER TOR SPREE

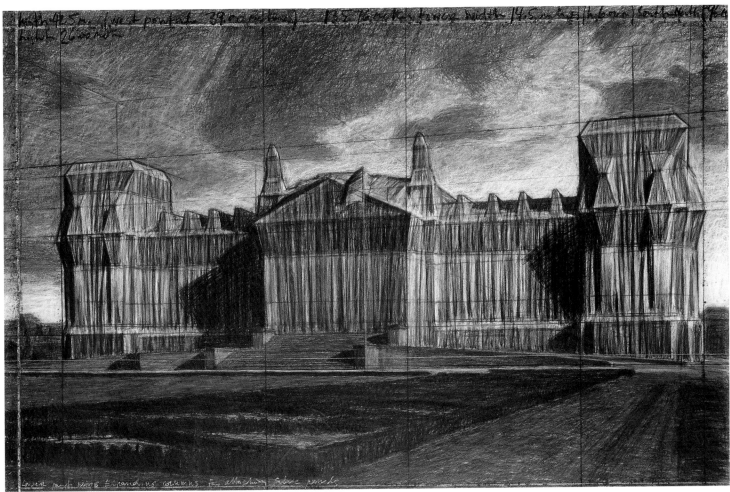

ical processes invariably involved in their projects comes the moment of recognition – the magical awareness of the transformation aptly described by Dieter Ronte, Director of the Bonn Kunstmuseum: "For a brief moment, the artist wants to withdraw [the Reichstag] from our sight by changing its functional context. The building is to become sculpture, a formulated esthetic. At the end of which it will be transformed back again. After its unveiling it is to stand before us freshly innocent." The Christos' is an art of knowing innocence, an art of sophisticated simplicity, and above all, for all the technical intricacy that goes into its realization, an art of wonder.

Wrapped Reichstag, Project for Berlin
Drawings, 1994, in two parts
Pencil, charcoal, pastel, crayon, technical
data, map and fabric sample,
38 x 165 cm and 106.6 x 165 cm
New York, Collection Jeanne-Claude Christo

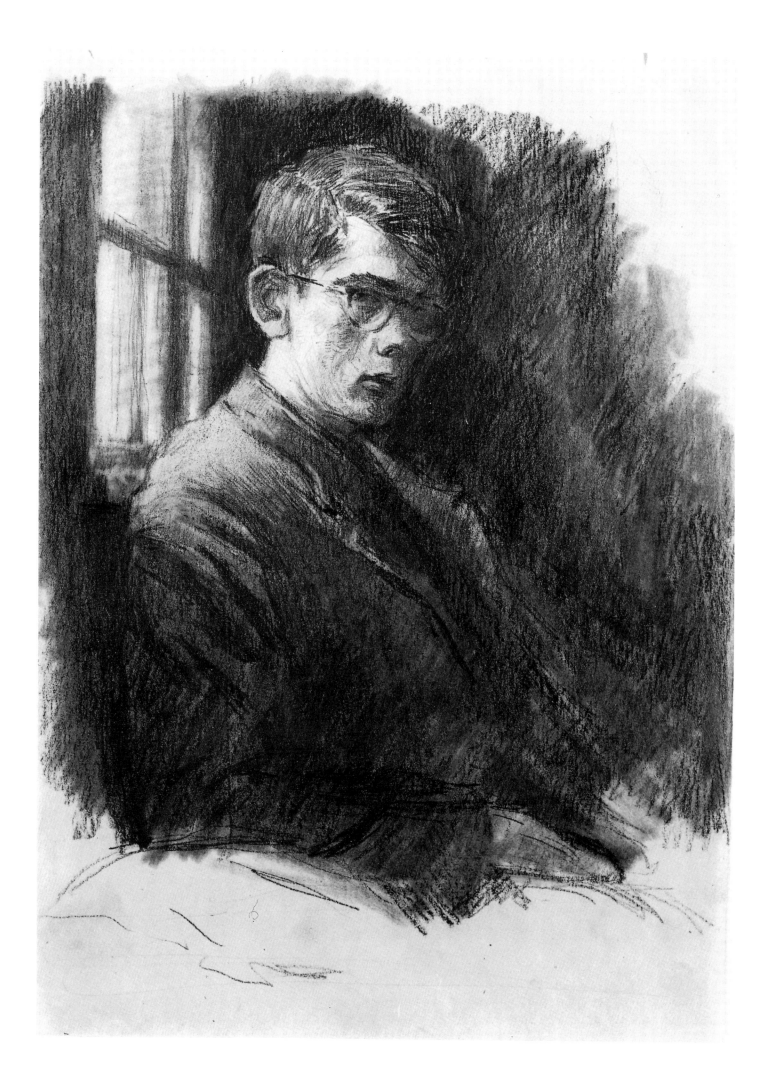

"Miserable autumn weekends"
Out of Bulgaria

Christo Vladimiroff Javacheff was born on June 13, 1935, in Gabrovo, an industrial town in the north of Bulgaria – the very same day and year, amazingly, that Jeanne-Claude was born in Casablanca. Christo's father owned a chemicals factory established in Gabrovo by his grandfather, who was of Czech-Bulgarian origin; his mother, Tzveta Dimitrova, who was Secretary General of the Sofia Academy of Fine Arts until her marriage in 1931, had fled Macedonia for Bulgaria following Turkish massacres. "Our mother," Anani, Christo's older brother, told *Balkan Magazine* (IX, 1993), "had to flee Macedonia with our grandmother in 1913. Grandmother was a troublemaker in Salonika, where she lived. Our grandfather was a big merchant in Salonika – the Turks killed him in 1913, on an island together with other people. My grandmother was left alone, and had three children on her hands: a two-month-old boy and two girls. The house was surrounded by the Turks. She was inside the house together with the children. The Turks brought artillery and started firing on the house. The family survived somehow, escaped death, and on the next day, or God knows after how many days, managed to get on board a British ship that had just arrived. My grandmother was disguised as a Turkish woman, with her three kids and a sewing-machine, which she managed to carry. She finally arrived safely at Dedeagaç, and from there to Sofia. My mother was seven years old then. It was in Sofia that my mother later went to high school."

Christo's family, which included an elder brother, Anani (now a well-known actor in Bulgaria) and a younger, Stefan (now a chemist), saw out the Second World War in a relatively secure country house that was a haven for artists and other friends fleeing the Allied bombing of the cities. Christo's childhood memories included the corpses of partisans executed in the streets, and the entrance of the Red Army into Bulgaria in 1944.

Christo's father, a western-educated scientist, was harassed and hounded by the new Communist regime. His chemicals factory was nationalized under the Communists, and the teenaged Christo visited his father, now branded a "saboteur", in prison. To *Balkan Magazine*, Christo recalled the early 1950s as a time of "frenzy and upheaval. Everything slowed down and decadence set in."

By the time he was twelve, Christo already knew about the Reichstag, since it played a key role in Bulgarian Communist lore: Georgi Dimitrov, Prime Minister of Bulgaria in the late 1940s, had been a defendant (later acquitted) in the Reichstag fire trial in 1933. Christo himself was a quiet, gentle youngster, shy of girls and vulnerable to ridicule. "I was restless, frantic," remembers Christo's brother Anani, "while he was always at mother's side. He was her favorite one. He always used to tell mother, Tzveta was her name, that they would never part... she suffered much

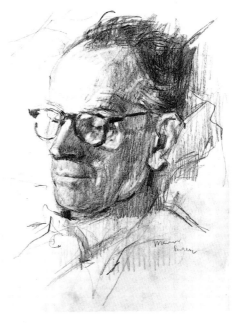

Vladimir Javacheff, the Artist's Father Resting, 1952
Pencil on paper, 24.5 x 18.5 cm
New York, Collection Jeanne-Claude Christo

PAGE 12:
Self-Portrait, 1951
Pencil on paper, 51.5 x 41.9 cm
New York, Collection Jeanne-Claude Christo

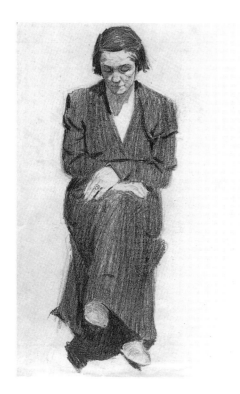

Tzveta, the Artist's Mother, 1948
Pencil on paper, 48.5 x 31.5 cm
New York, Collection Jeanne-Claude Christo

when developments in Hungary took place, and Christo went over to Prague and later reached Vienna." Christo himself recalls the beautiful house in Gabrovo with fondness, and the village, too, where the family used to spend the summer. "The family got acquainted with a village woman who brought us butter and cheese during the war. We became very good friends, and every summer went over there. We assisted with the household and farm work. We tended the sheep, harvested fruit, and so spent the whole summer."

Christo's earliest ventures in art dated back to that village, too, where "there was a woman who was born without arms. She used to do so many things, almost everything, with her feet. She taught herself to do so – even knitted with her feet. At the age of six I made her and others sit for me, so I could paint their portraits." In 1953 he began his formal training at the Academy in the Bulgarian capital, Sofia. There he studied painting, sculpture, architecture and design until 1956. Socialist realism was the order of the day, and the agitprop approach prevalent throughout the Communist bloc dictated a propagandist, Marxist-Leninist treatment of subject matter and style in art.

The kinds of grotesque lengths Christo's generation had to go to have often been described. The route of the Orient Express, for instance, lay through Bulgaria; and students were therefore sent to agricultural co-operatives (on "miserable autumn weekends") to advise farmers along the track how to show off their tractors or haystacks to the best advantage, to impress travellers from capitalist countries. This propaganda work was mandatory to obtain course credit. Still, something more valuable in his later life may have remained with Christo from those curious exercises: his communicative skill, and his sense of art's physical dimension in landscape, may derive in part from such experience.

He fell foul of socialist realism, and Professor Panayotov's Academy dictates, with a composition that showed peasants in a cornfield (p. 15), resting instead of working. One was drinking; the soil looked unproductive; and

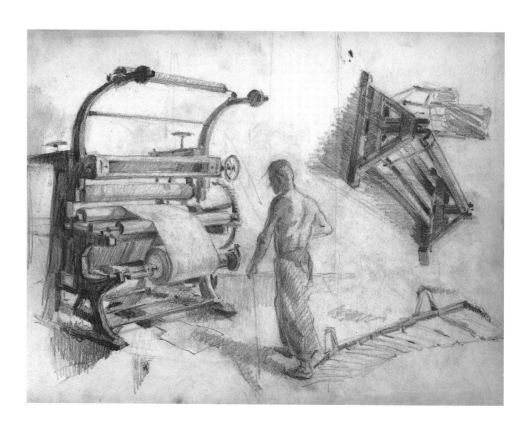

Textile machinery in Plovdiv factory, 1950
Pencil on paper, 40 x 54 cm
New York, Collection Jeanne-Claude Christo

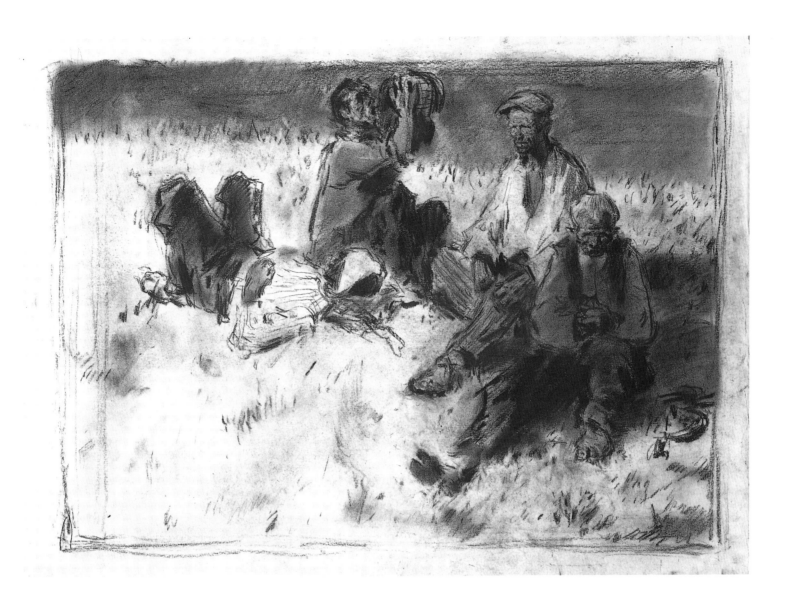

even the violet and green shirts of the peasants met with disapproval.
Christo was defying the system. How dare he be so provocative?

Bulgaria was the most ardently Stalinist nation in the Communist bloc,
the isolated hinterland of Europe, and Christo knew that if he was ever to
see work by Matisse or Picasso, Klee or Kandinsky, anywhere outside the
covers of a book, he would have to go west. His dream was of Paris, but his
first stop was Prague, where for the first time he saw originals by the great
moderns. Then on January 10, 1956, with eighteen others, Christo bribed a
frontier guard on the Czech border, and made good his passage by train to
Vienna. With neither money nor any knowledge of the language, Christo
took a taxi to the only address he knew in Vienna, that of a friend of his
father. The address was thirty-five years old, but the friend still lived there
and took Christo in, and the next morning the young Bulgarian hurried off to
enrol at the Vienna Academy of Fine Arts. Matriculation as a student by-
passed the need to register as a refugee. Fritz Wotruba was head of the
Vienna sculpture department, and Robert Anderson was Christo's professor
at the academy, but he stayed for one semester only, moving first to Geneva
(where he painted portraits of society ladies and children in order to survive)
and from there to Paris.

Farmers at Rest in a Field (study for an oil
painting), 1954
Charcoal on paper, 35 x 50 cm
New York, Collection Jeanne-Claude Christo

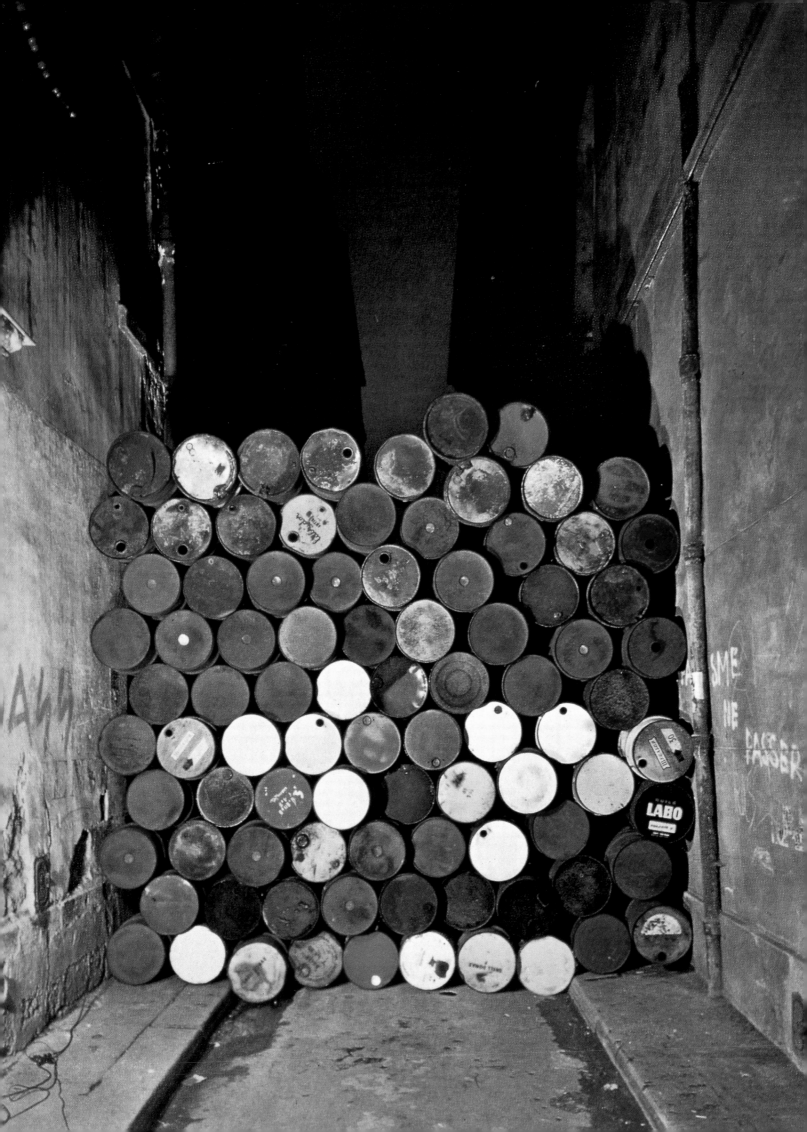

"Revelation through concealment"
Paris

Christo arrived in Paris in March 1958 and took a tiny room on the Ile Saint-Louis, and, as studio, a maid's room on Rue de Saint-Sénoch. He continued to make a living painting portraits (signed Javacheff), and his work impressed René Bourgeois, a society hairdresser, who recommended him to the wife of General de Guillebon. De Guillebon was a French war hero who had led the troops that liberated Paris and later taken Berchtesgaden, where Hitler had his Berghof and Adlerhorst retreats. His daughter Jeanne-Claude met Christo when he came to the family home to paint her mother (in three versions – plain realist, Impressionist, and Cubist) and was soon in love with the penniless Bulgarian refugee. Her family considered him gifted but an unsuitable match: "they wanted Christo as a son, not a son-in-law," Jeanne-Claude told *Avenue Magazine* in 1990. But she and Christo were soon living together and later married, with Christo's friend Pierre Restany, the critic and founder of the *Nouveaux Réalistes* movement, acting as best man at the wedding. "I could tell you it was the art," Jeanne-Claude told *Avenue*, "but actually he was a hell of a lover."

Christo's move west had been a serious upheaval in his life, one he had countenanced because conditions in which creative work had to operate behind the Iron Curtain were stifling. In choosing the freedom every artist needs, he was not without personal courage; but finding out what it was he had to do (as he himself puts it), locating his authentic vein and genuine self, mattered above all else. In Paris he now took two further steps that changed his life as an artist.

The first was simple: he shed his Slavic surname, Javacheff, and henceforth used only his first name, Christo, the name by which he is now known worldwide, for his art.

The second change, dating almost from the beginning of his time in Paris, touched upon the substance of his art. He began to wrap. Christo wrapped cans, bottles, chairs, a car – anything he could find, everyday objects of no particular beauty or interest. Resembling the Pop artists in this respect (and also, later, in his skilful use of press and the media for his own purposes), he implicitly assumed that any object could be worthy of the attentions of art: there were no hierarchies or distinctions any more. He wrapped his chosen objects in canvas and tied them securely with string, rope or twine. He even painted some of them.

Over the next few years he continued to wrap a bewildering variety of objects – chairs, a wheelbarrow, a motorcycle, naked women, oil barrels (of which we shall have more to say), and a Volkswagen car. On occasion he juxtaposed items: *Wrapped Cans and Bottles* (1958–1959) included several wrapped bottles and cans alongside a few unwrapped painted cans, and bottles containing red pigment.

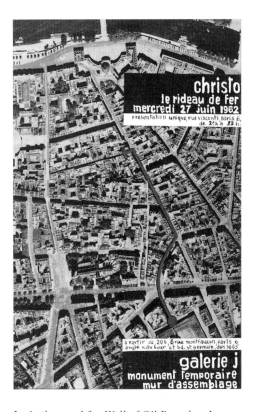

Invitation card for *Wall of Oil Barrels – Iron Curtain (Le Rideau de Fer)*, 1962
New York, Collection Jacob Baal-Teshuva

PAGE 16:
Wall of Oil Barrels – Iron Curtain,
Rue Visconti, Paris, June 27, 1962
Oil barrels, 4.3 x 3.8 x 1.7 m

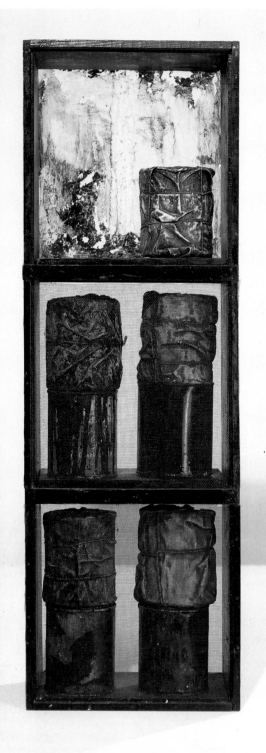

Shelves, 1958
Five wrapped cans and four cans on three shelves: wood, glass, lacquered canvas, rope and paint, 90 x 30 x 18 cm
New York, Collection Jeanne-Claude Christo

PAGE 19:
Wrapped Oil Barrels, 1958–1959
Fabric, enamel paint, steel wire and barrels
Barrels range in size from: 49 x 33 cm to 89 x 59 cm
New York, Collection Jeanne-Claude Christo

The wrapping of small objects that could be transformed into limited editions for a collectors' market was to be of considerable importance in Christo's future career, since it became an important source of income and thus of the funding needed for projects that became ever larger and costlier. Thus in the 1960s there were editions of wrapped magazines (p. 26); of a *Wrapped Flower* (this was not in fact published by George Maciunas at the time and was found in his archives after his death in 1978); of *Wrapped Roses* (in 1968, on the occasion of Christo's exhibition at the Institute of Contemporary Art in Philadelphia, to help cover expenses incurred by his mastaba there – and, in the same year, an edition from Richard Feigen Graphics in New York); a *Wrapped Painting* in 1969; a wrapped model of Cologne cathedral, done together with German artist Klaus Staeck in 1969; prints of wrapped trees in 1970 (the first life-size *Wrapped Tree* dating from 1966 in Holland); and so forth. Occasionally these small-scale objects have been given away for purposes of good relations, but more usually they have attracted collectors who want lasting mementoes, and have played a part, however indirect, in making Christo's larger-scale projects possible.

The principle of wrapping, covering, and concealing (yet not entirely disguising) allowed for surprising versatility. Works such as the *Package on Table* (1961, p. 25), *Wrapped Chair* (1961) or *Wrapped Motorcycle* (1962) might be clad in semi-transparent materials instead of (or in addition to) opaque fabric. Objects might be only partially masked; or, of course, they might be entirely enveloped so that the content was neither visible nor recognizable (*Package*, 1961, p. 25). For the principle at stake in this process, witless to hostile critics and enchanting in the eyes of Christo's supporters, David Bourdon found the perfect formula, in a biography published in 1970: "revelation through concealment".

That is indeed the key. Christo touches the world with wonder. From those modest beginnings in Paris he has gone on, over a career of thirty-five years, to wrap everything – from tin cans to a stretch of Australian coastline – and has created a body of work that, as we shall see, has gone far beyond wrapping, retaining only the use of fabric as a common denominator. His work has afforded "one of the eeriest visual spectacles of our time" (Bourdon), and has made the Christos celebrities on the international stage. Not that fame in itself is of interest: but theirs is the reward for an unusual steadiness of vision.

During Christo's French years, the Paris art scene was dominated by the *Nouveaux Réalistes*, the group of New Realists founded in 1960 by Pierre Restany. Christo's membership of this group is sometimes disputed, not least by the artist himself. The eight founder members of the group, signatories to the original manifesto, were Yves Klein, Martial Raysse, François Dufrêne, Raymond Hains, Jacques de la Villeglé, Jean Tinguely, Arman and Daniel Spoerri. Others who subsequently became associated with the group – Gérard Deschamps, Mimmo Rotella, Niki de Saint-Phalle, César, and Christo himself – never in fact signed the Paris Manifesto. Though he was not formally invited to join, Christo exhibited at the group's 1963 show in Munich, and later in Milan. Pierre Restany has claimed that this signalled his membership. Christo denies that this was so, and Bourdon noted that Christo's "involvement was marginal and brief"; but Christo is now widely considered one of the thirteen members of the *Nouveaux Réalistes*, and indeed exhibited with the group at a much later date, in Nice (July – September 1981) and at the Musée d'Art Moderne de la Ville de Paris (May – September 1986).

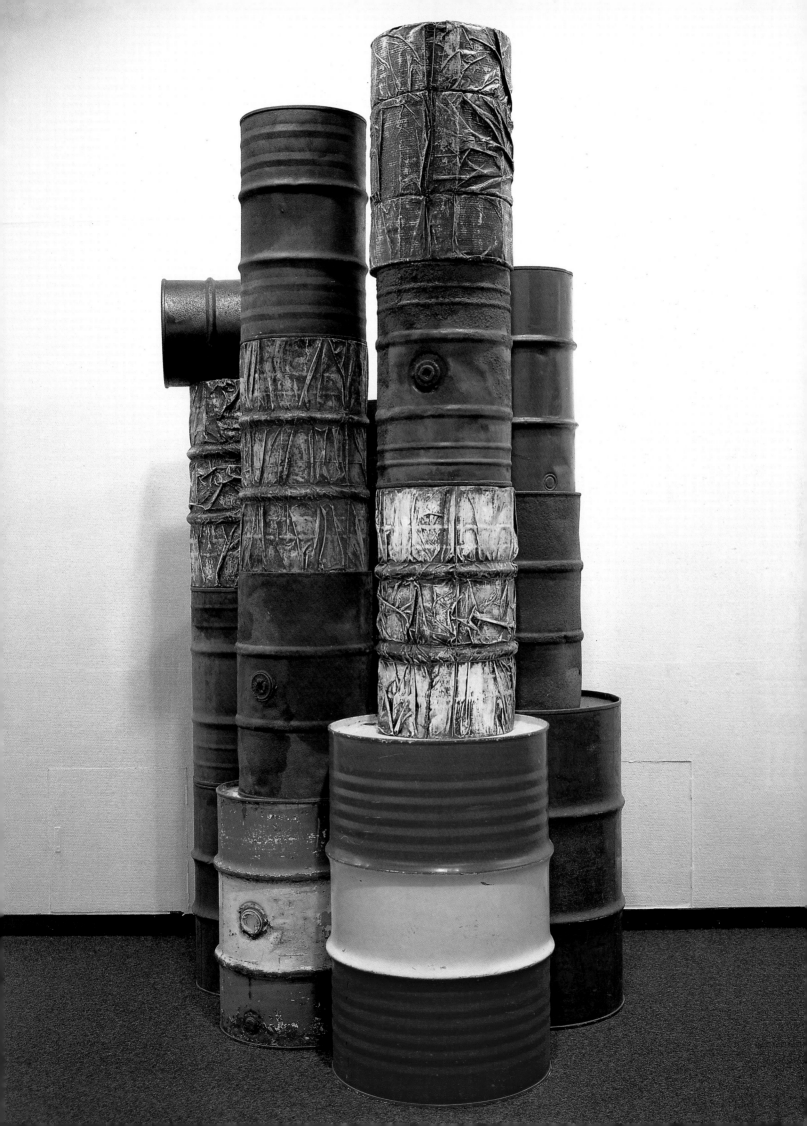

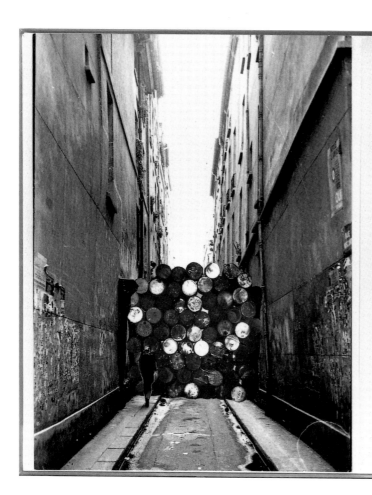

*Project for a Temporary Wall of oil Barrels,
Rue Visconti, Paris*
Collage, 1961
Two photographs and a typewritten text,
24 x 40.5 cm
New York, Collection Jeanne-Claude Christo

"Rue Visconti is a one-way street, between Rue Bonaparte and Rue de Seine, 140 meters long and with an average width of 3 meters. The street ends at number 25 on the left side and at 26 on the right. It has few shops: a bookstore, a modern art gallery, an antiques shop, an electrical supplies shop, a grocery store. At the corner of Rue Visconti and Rue de Seine, the Cabaret du Petit More (or Maure) was opened in 1618. The poet Saint-Amant, an assiduous customer, died there. The art gallery that now stands on the site of the tavern has fortunately retained the façade and the seventeenth-century sign, as described on page 134 of Rocheguide/Clébert: Promenades dans les rues de Paris, Rive Gauche, Editions Denoël.
The Wall will be built between numbers 1 and 2, completely closing the street to traffic, and will cut all communication between Rue Bonaparte and Rue de Seine. […] This Iron Curtain can be used as a barricade during a period of public work in the street, or to transform the street into a dead end. Finally its principle can be extended to a whole area or an entire city.
CHRISTO, Paris, October 1961"

Be that as it may, it was in an art climate created by the *Nouveaux Realistes* that Christo first wrapped objects and engaged on his earliest oil barrel projects. He was also exhibiting: in 1961 he had his first one-person show at the Haro Lauhus Gallery in Cologne, where he exhibited his first outdoor barrel structures. Cologne at that time was already developing the lively art scene for which it is now known, and Christo met John Cage, Nam June Paik and Mary Bauermeister there, as well as his first collector, industrialist Dieter Rosenkranz. The *Dockside Packages* (1961, p. 22) and *Stacked Oil Barrels* were created in and for Cologne parallel to his exhibition. The former, on the Cologne riverfront, consisted of several heaps of cardboard barrels and industrial paper rolls covered with tarpaulins and secured with rope; the latter was precisely described by its title (the barrels lying on their sides). Both works were made by simply rearranging material already available at Cologne's Rhine docks.

David Bourdon observed in his biography of Christo that the large assemblages of oil drums he erected along the Cologne waterfront were hardly distinguishable from the stockpiles that are found in harbors everywhere – but Christo had in fact composed his materials, and had used hoists, cranes and tractors to arrange them as he required. This touches upon the very heart of what is sometimes seen as a minimalist element in Christo's artistic approach. Traditionally, artists declare themselves free both in their selection from given reality and in their skill at handling their chosen material; the Christos, throughout their careers, have always challenged this conception, by their great readiness to accept what is given and subject it to little alteration.

1961 was also, of course, the year in which, on August 13, the Wall was built by East Berlin's Communist regime. A stateless man with no passport, himself a refugee from a Communist country, Christo was deeply affected

Project for a Wrapped Public Building, 1961
Collaged photographs by Harry Shunk and a
text by Christo, 41.5 x 25 cm
New York, Collection Jeanne-Claude Christo

"I. General Notes:
The building is in a huge and symmetrical site.
A building with a rectangular base, without
any façade. The building will be completely
closed – that is, wrapped on all sides. Access
will be underground, with entrances placed at
15 or 20 meters from the building. The wrapping of the building will be performed with
sheets of tarpaulin and sheets of reinforced
plastic of an average width of 10 to 20 meters,
and with metal cables and ordinary ropes.
With the cables we can obtain the points
which can then be used to wrap the building.
The cables make scaffolding unnecessary. To
obtain the required result, some 10,000 meters
of tarpaulin, 20,000 meters of cable and
80,000 meters of rope will be needed.
This project for a wrapped public building can
be used:
I. As a sports hall with swimming-pools, football stadium and Olympic stadium or as a skat-
ing or ice-hockey rink.
II. As a concert hall, planetarium, conference
hall or as an experimental testing-site.
III. As a historical museum, or as a museum
of art ancient or modern.
IV. As a parliamentary hall or as a prison.
CHRISTO
October 1961, Paris"

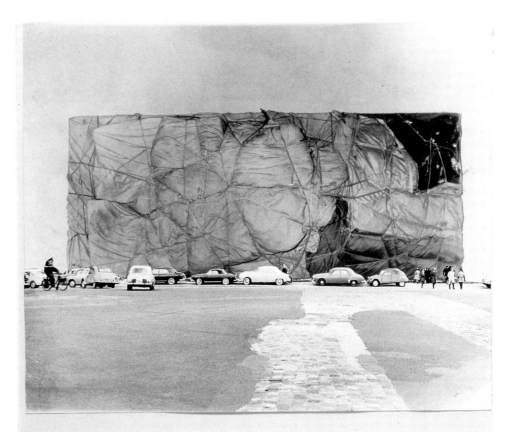

PROJET DE UN EDIFICE PUBLIC EMPAQUETE

I. Notes générales:
Il s'agit d'un immeuble situé dans un empla-
cement vaste et régulier.
Un bâtiment ayant une base rectangulaire, sans
aucune façade. Le bâtiment sera complètement
fermé-c'est à dire empaqueté de tous les cô-
tés. Les entrées seront souterraines, placées
environ à 15 ou 20 metres de cet edifice.
L'empaquetage de cet immeuble sera éxécuté
avec des bâches des toiles gommées et des
toiles de matiere plastique renforcée d'un
largeur mouenne de 10 à 20 metres, des cordes
métalliques et ordinaires. Avec les cordes
de métal nous pouvons obtenir les points,
qui peuvent servir en suite à l'empaquetage
de bâtiment. Les cordes métalliques évitent
la construction d'un échafaudage. Pour obtenir le resultat nécessaire il faut environ
10000 metres de bâches, 20000 metres de
cordes métalliques, 80000 metres de cordes
ordinaires.
Le present projet pour un edifice public
empaqueté est utilisable:
I.Comme salle sportive-avec des piscines,
le stade de football, le stade des disci-
plines olimpiques, ou soit comme patinoire
à glace ou à hockey.
II.Comme salle de concert, planetarium, salle de conférence et essais expérimentaux.
III.Comme un musée historique, d'art anci-
éne et d'art moderne.
IV.Comme salle parlementaire ou un prison.

CHRISTO
octobre 1961, Paris

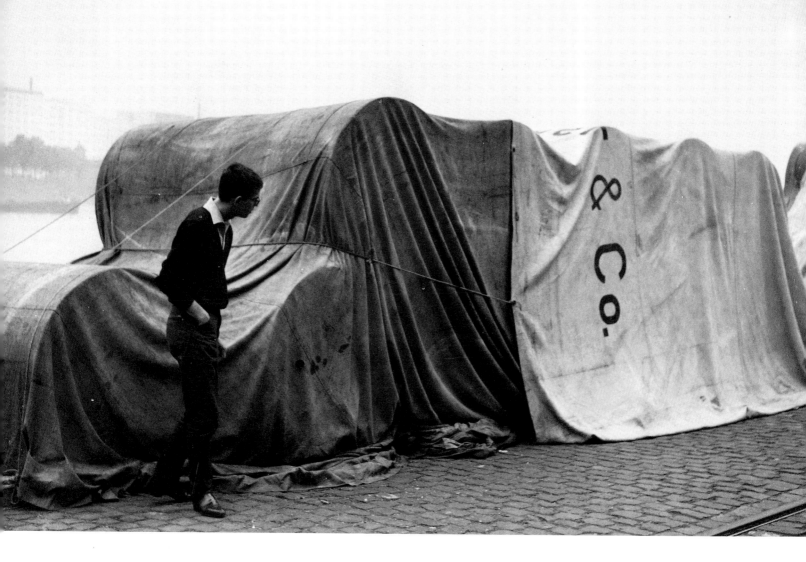

Christo standing in front of his *Dockside Packages (Cologne Harbor)*, 1961

Dockside Packages (Cologne Harbor)
(detail), 1961
Rolls of paper, tarpaulin and rope,
480 x 180 x 960 cm

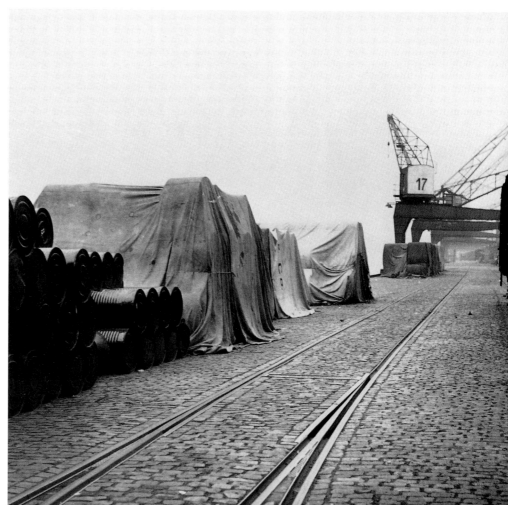

22

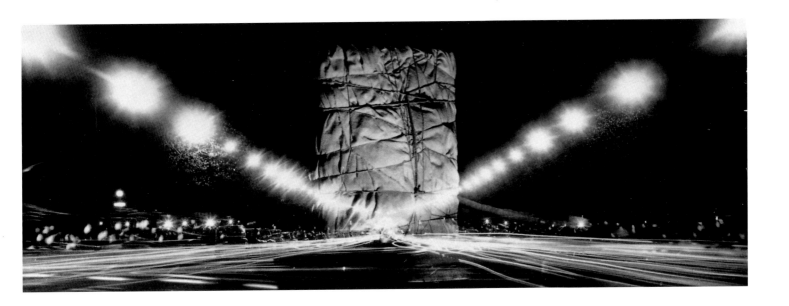

and angered by the East German move. On his return to Paris from Cologne in October 1961 he began preparing his personal response to the building of the wall. This was the *Wall of Oil Barrels – Iron Curtain* (1961–1962, p. 16); the Christos proposed to block Rue Visconti, a narrow one-way street on the Left Bank, with 204 oil barrels, and prepared a detailed description of the project (p. 20).

The preparation of written documentation, accompanied by photocollages and logistical analysis, has become ever more complex over the years as the Christos' projects have become more demanding and ambitious, but the purposes served by these documents have remained essentially constant: to persuade the relevant authorities to give permission for a project to proceed, to publicize and define the nature of a project, and, as commentators have pointed out, to deflect critics' attention from esthetic evaluation towards the examination of technical, social or environmental data. In the case of the *Wall of Oil Barrels – The Iron Curtain* project (p. 16) the document failed in its first purpose: permission was refused. (Years later, in New York, when the Christos proposed to close 53rd Street with 441 barrels to mark the end of the Dada and Surrealism exhibition at the Museum of Modern Art on June 8, 1968, he was again out of luck: various city authorities refused to grant them the necessary permission.)

Undeterred, the Christos went ahead with their *Wall of Oil Barrels – The Iron Curtain* project without permission. For eight hours on June 27, 1962, they blocked the Rue Visconti – at various times the home of Racine, Delacroix and Balzac – with 204 oil drums. Christo carried every one himself; the armies of helpers, both professional and unskilled, who were to become so familiar a feature of the spectacular art projects in later years were conspicuous by their absence on this occasion. The barricade, measuring 4.3 by 3.8 by 1.7 meters, obstructed the traffic as predicted. The oil barrels were left in their found state, in their industrial colors, complete with brand names and rust.

The Christos were inevitably summoned to the police station to answer for the obstruction, but no case was ever pursued. Whether the barricade was understood by casual passers-by to refer to the Berlin Wall is a debatable point; at that time there were frequent demonstrations in Paris in protest against the Algerian war, and permission may even have been refused because officials mistook the project for a protest on that issue. But the

Wrapped Building, Project (detail), 1963
Photomontage
New York, Collection Jeanne-Claude Christo

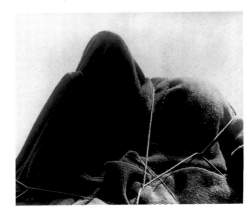

Man Ray
The Enigma of Isidore Ducasse, 1920
Photograph
Paris, Collection Lucien Treillard

Henry Moore
Crowd Looking at a Tied-up Object, 1942
Chalk, crayon, watercolor, pen and ink on paper, 43.2 x 55.9 cm
Collection The Late Lord Clark of Saltwood, Courtesy the Henry Moore Foundation

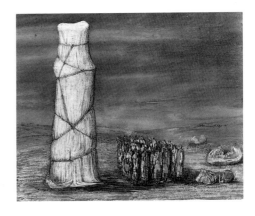

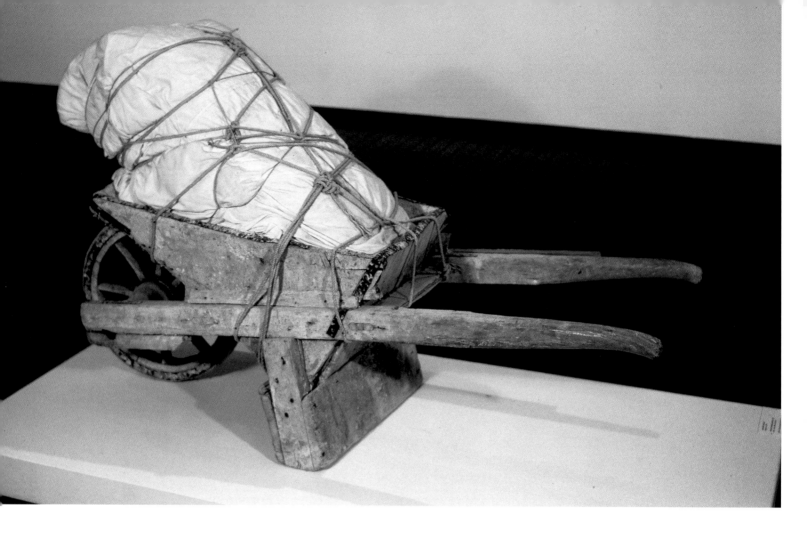

Package on Wheelbarrow, 1963
Cloth, wood, rope, metal and wooden wheelbarrow, 89 x 152.5 x 58.5cm
New York, The Museum of Modern Art

PAGE 25 LEFT:
Package on Table, 1961
Wood, fabric and ropes, 124 x 61.5 x 30cm
New York, Collection Jeanne-Claude Christo

PAGE 25 RIGHT:
Wrapped Road Signs, 1963
Wooden road signs, steel stand, lantern, chain, fabric, rope and jute, 181 x 62.5 x 47cm
New York, Collection Jeanne-Claude Christo

PAGE 25 BOTTOM:
Package, 1961
Fabric and rope on wood, 84 x 137 x 20.3cm
New York, Collection Jeanne-Claude Christo

Christos had made a breakthrough nonetheless in terms of public art, by using a street, oil barrels, and even the presence of people in the street – given features never previously considered admissible in art – to create a temporary work. Crucial to the Christos' post-modern approach to art has always been this emphasis on the temporary.

Christo's ambition extended to large-scale projects at a very early date. In 1961 he made his first study for a *Wrapped Public Building* (p. 21), collaging photographs and preparing a written account: "The building is in a huge and symmetrical site. A building with a rectangular base, without any façade. The building will be completely closed – that is, wrapped on all sides. Access will be underground, with entrances placed at 15 or 20 meters from the building. The wrapping of the building will be performed with sheets of tarpaulin and sheets of reinforced plastic of an average width of 10 to 20 meters, and with metal cables and ordinary ropes." Soon Christo was making his first proposals to wrap specific public buildings – the Ecole Militaire in Paris, and the Arc de Triomphe – but none of these projects was ever realized. The wrapping of the Ecole Militaire was to involve covering the building with tarpaulins, using steel cables and strong manila rope. (The steel cables would obviate the need for scaffolding.) The wrapping (Christo explained in his project description) could be used as protection during maintenance work such as repair or cleaning of walls; for a parliament or a jail; or as package scaffolding if the building were ever to be demolished. The wariness of the authorities in the face of such proposals was plainly connected with an inability to decide how seriously to take the artist.

There are few precedents for Christo's interest in wrapping. Henry Moore's drawing *Crowd Looking at a Tied-up Object* (1942, p. 23) and Man Ray's photograph *The Enigma of Isidore Ducasse* (1920, p. 23), showing a

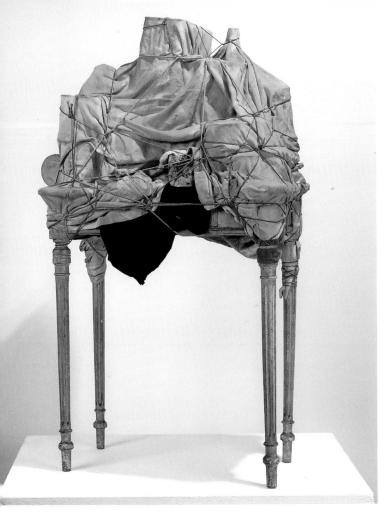
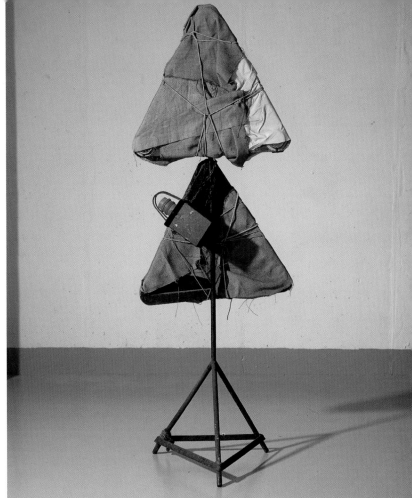
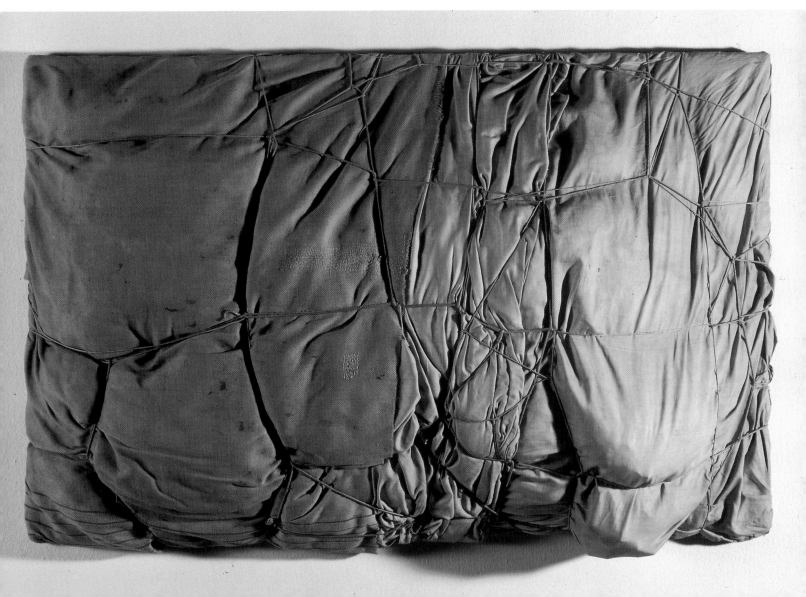

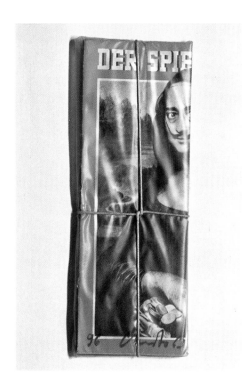

Der Spiegel Magazine Wrapped, 1963
Magazine, polyethylene and rope, 30 x 13 x 2.5 cm
New York, Collection Jeanne-Claude Christo

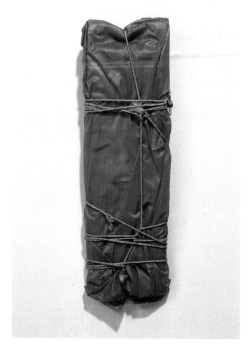

Wrapped Magazine, 1963
Magazine, polyethylene and rope, 40 x 13 x 3.5 cm
New York, Collection Jeanne-Claude Christo

PAGE 27:
Wrapped Portrait of Jeanne-Claude, 1963
Oil painting wrapped in polyethylene and rope, 75 x 55 x 4 cm
New York, Collection Jeanne-Claude Christo

wrapped sewing-machine, have been suggested as influences, but Christo replies that he did not discover these works till later in his career, after he had begun wrapping.

The issue scarcely seems pressing: even if we accept an affinity between aspects of Christo's work and the two earlier pieces, Christo has in any case long since moved beyond his legendary status in the press as "King of the Wrap", and many of the Christos' important later projects – the *Valley Curtain, Rifle, Colorado* (1970–1972, p. 40) or *Running Fence* (1972–1976, p. 50), the *Surrounded Islands* (1980–1983, p. 56) or *The Umbrellas, Japan and USA* (1984–1991, p. 72/73) – merely retain the interest in using fabric.

And in *Over the River* too, a current project looking beyond the Reichstag wrapping, the emphasis is not on wrapping but on enhancement, on the creation of new shapes and images using the natural environment together with effects of fabric, motion and light.

The Christos' esthetic, as told to the present writer, is a distinctive one: "Traditional sculpture creates its own space. We take a space not belonging to sculpture, and make sculpture out of it.
It's similar to what Claude Monet did with the cathedral at Rouen. Claude Monet was not saying that the Gothic cathedral was good or bad, but he could see the cathedral in blue, yellow and purple."

In evolving this esthetic, the Christos have invested immense resources of energy, resources directed (as we have seen) at locating their genuine selves. Much of this energy has to do with their displaced status; it is no accident that they have made their home in the great melting-pot, the USA. "In 1964," Christo told *Balkan Magazine*, "I already knew I had to go to America because over there things were already evolving. As early as 1962 in Paris, the famous art dealer Leo Castelli told me my place was in America." As they kept moving, the Christos were forever seeking, and forever finding.

And what they found, above all else, was a means to creation that satisfied the wise dictum of G. K. Chesterton: "Every work of art has one indispensable mark: the centre of it is simple, however much the fulfilment may be complicated." Critics well or ill disposed whose concern is with the logistics of the Christos' art would do well to bear this in mind.

Esthetically speaking, one other issue needs addressing, since the Christos' reliance on the beauties of a creation with no meanings beyond the thing itself implies an indifference to conceptions that see art as having a role (social, political, moral or philosophical) beyond itself. Or, to put it differently: if the Christos are content for the artwork to "be" rather than to "mean", does that not place them in the art-for-art's-sake camp? The notion of art for art's sake, originated by the French writer Victor Cousin (1792–1867), has fallen into disrepute in recent decades, since it implies a narcissistic disdain for life as it is lived and experienced by most people.

The doctrine is associated with the priestly caste of artists, writers and thinkers of the later nineteenth and early twentieth centuries (such as Mallarmé or Nietzsche, Gustave Moreau or Stefan George) who held themselves aloof from common life and tended to have right-wing political ideas that in some cases (Ezra Pound) did not even stop short of fascism. If it is correct to see the Christos as sharing some of the art-for-art's-sake convictions, it is also important to point out that their brand of populism always insists on the pleasure of ordinary people, rather than excluding them: the implications of art for art's sake are complex, and we should beware of suggesting that the Christos endorse any of them except the love of beauty in the artwork, regardless of social or moral or other affiliations.

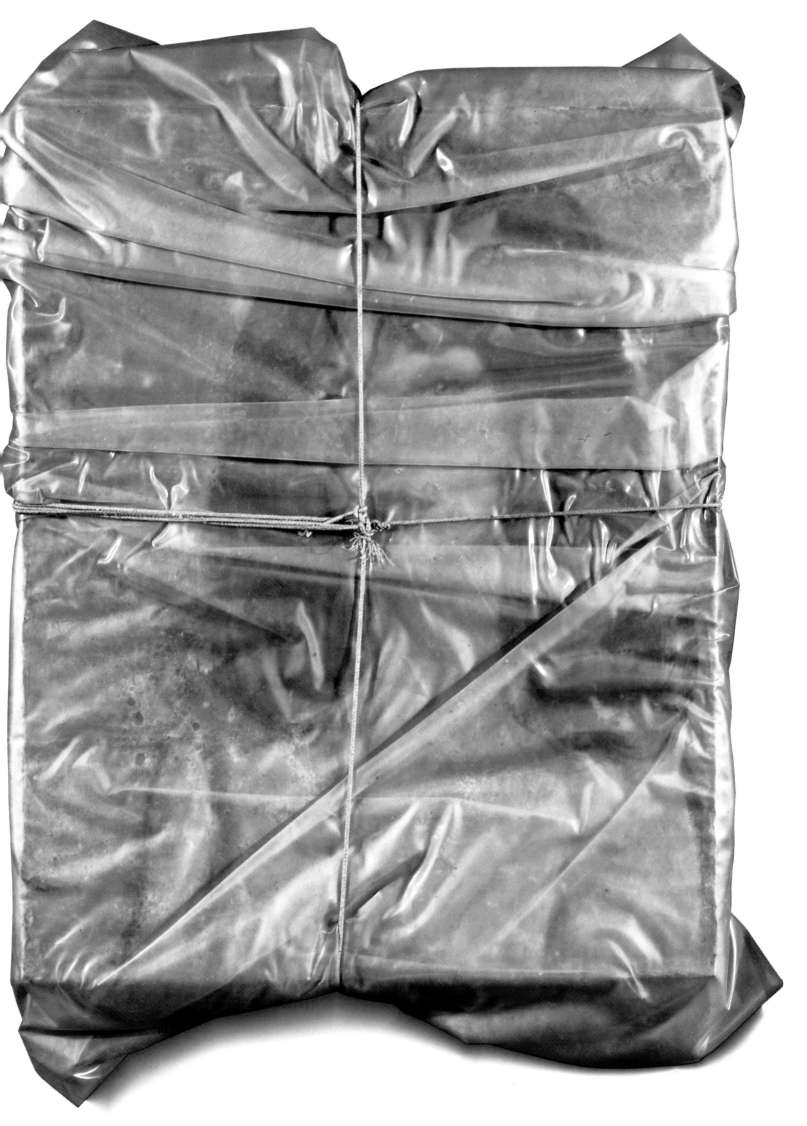

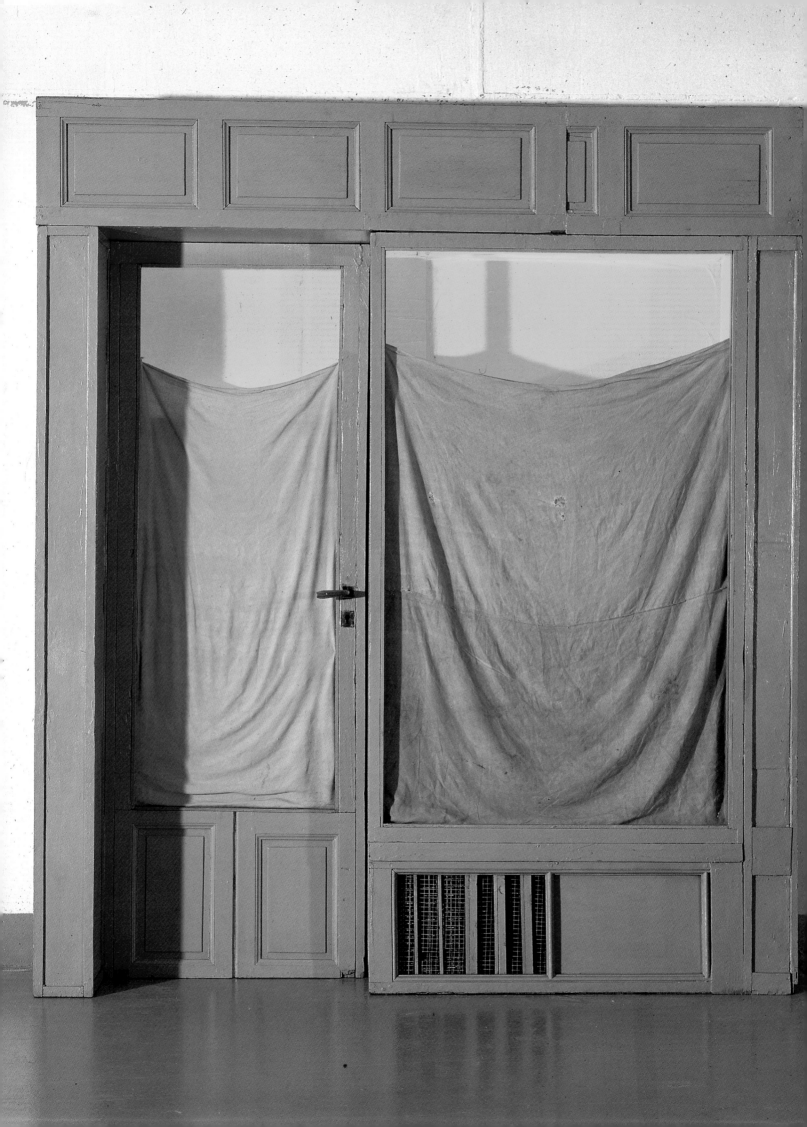

"Tributes to artistic freedom"

Store Fronts, Air Packages, Wrapped Museums

1964 marked another new beginning in their life, as Christo and Jeanne-Claude and their four-year-old son Cyril made the move Castelli had urged, the move to the city that had now superseded Paris as the world's art capital: New York. They first stayed at the Chelsea Hotel, the famed home-from-home for artists, writers and composers. Before long, the Christos were living in a downtown loft, which they fixed with money borrowed from the hotel. As collateral for their debt at the Chelsea they left the owner, Stanley Bard, one of the Store Front projects Christo had embarked on in New York. The debt was cleared in eight months, but the work remained at the Chelsea on loan, and in due course, some twenty years later, the Christos and the hotel proprietor agreed to donate it to the Israel Museum in Jerusalem.

The *Store Fronts*, the first of which Christo built at the Chelsea, were shop façades made of wood and painted in a variety of colors – each project preceded by preparatory artefacts, drawings and collages. They can be seen as a continuation of the glass show-cases the artist worked on in Paris before his departure for New York. Christo used fabric or wrapping paper (or both) to mask the inside of the display windows and glass doors; at times an electric light was placed inside. The result was enigmatic, architectonically elusive, evocative: the *Store Fronts* were of great beauty, possessed of a quiet melancholy and a sense of loneliness that recalled the work of the American painter Edward Hopper, or the boxes of Joseph Cornell. Their pervasive sense of mystery left the observer wondering what was behind the façades. The materials Christo used were plexiglass, old doors and wood found in the street, and, later, galvanized metal and aluminum. The *Green Store Front* has been exhibited in 1964 at Leo Castelli's Gallery in New York, and other storefronts were seen in the Stedelijk van Abbe Museum at Eindhoven in Holland. Christo continued these works for four years, and his largest, *Corridor Store Front*, was exhibited at Germany's *documenta IV* show in Kassel in 1968.

During the same period in the mid-1960s, Christo was making his three *Air Packages*, one of them being the largest inflated structure ever created without a support skeleton. The first was done for Christo's Eindhoven exhibition, and measured 5 meters in diameter. It was made of polyethylene, rubberized canvas, rope, steel cables – and, of course, air. The second, running to 1,200 cubic meters, was made at the Minneapolis School of Art in October 1966 by Christo and Jeanne-Claude with the assistance of 147 students (p.33).

The core of the air package consisted of four US Army high-altitude research balloons, independently sealed, each measuring about 550 centimeters in height and 762 centimeters in diameter. There were also 2,800 colored balloons of an average 70 centimeters in diameter. All the bal-

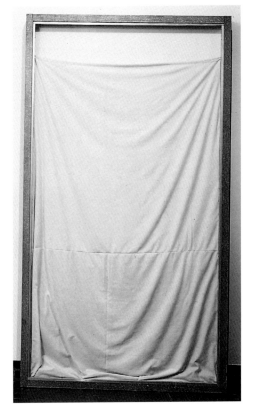

Show Window, 1965
Galvanized metal, plexiglas and fabric,
213.5 x 122 x 9.5 cm
New York, Collection Jeanne-Claude Christo

PAGE 28:
Purple Store Front, 1964
Wood, metal, enamel paint, fabric, plexiglas, paper and electric light, 235 x 220 x 35.3 cm
New York, Collection Jeanne-Claude Christo

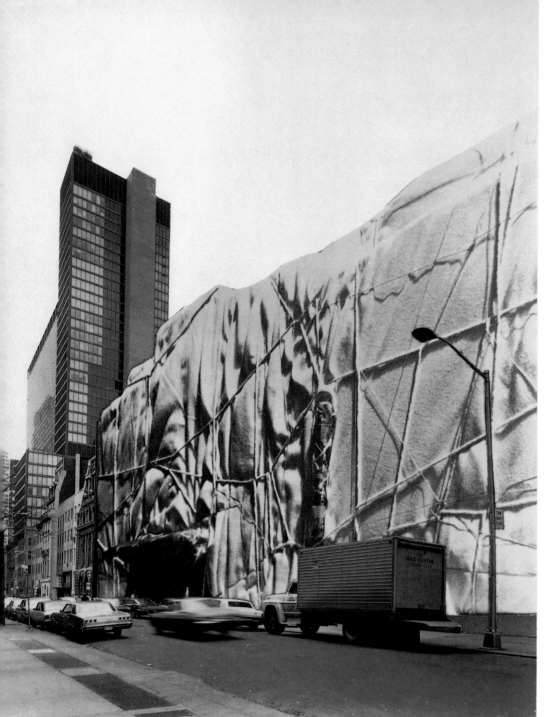

The Museum of Modern Art Wrapped,
Project for New York
Collaged photographs (detail), 1968
38 x 25.4 cm
New York, The Museum of Modern Art, Gift
of Mrs Dominique de Menil

Wrapped Whitney Museum of American Art,
Project for New York
Scale model, 1967
Fabric, twine, rope, polyethylene, wood and
paint, 51 x 49.5 x 56 cm
New York, Collection Jeanne-Claude Christo

loons were inflated, sealed, and then wrapped in 740 square meters of clear polyethylene, which was in turn sealed with Mylar tape and secured with 950 meters of manila rope. The resulting oblong package was further inflated by two air blowers.

Owing to air turbulence, the Aviation Agency vetoed the planned airlift, and the helicopter was permitted to lift the air package no more than 6 meters off the ground. The use of this helicopter was funded by Helen and David Johnson, collectors and friends of the Christos, in exchange for an original drawing. The remaining costs of the project were covered by an edition of one hundred *Wrapped Boxes*, which (in contrast to Christo's customary works) exactly resembled ordinary parcels. These were mailed to members of the Contemporary Arts Group, and those who inadvertently opened the boxes found inside a signed and numbered certificate reading: "You have just destroyed a work of art." In such gestures, Christo was wholly in line with the provocative, situationist mood of much progressive art in the mid-1960s.

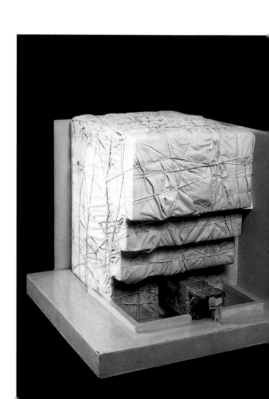

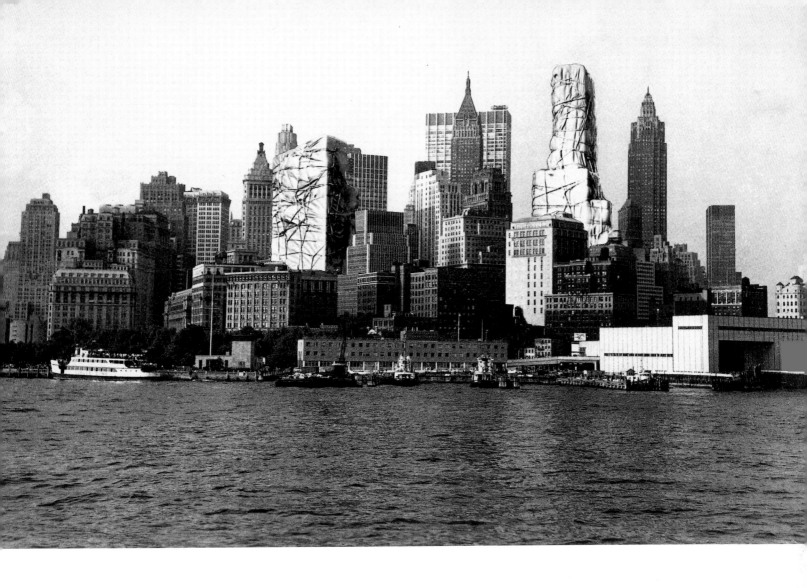

The third *Air Package* (1967–1968, p. 35), titled *5,600 Cubic Meter Package* (1960), which attracted the widest public attention, weighed in at 6,350 kilograms and consisted of an envelope of 2,000 square meters of trevira tied with rope. The heat-sealed envelope was contained in a net of 3.5 kilometers of rope prepared by professional riggers and secured with 1,200 knots. Other statistics might be added: the Christos' work invites analysis in terms of figures, and an account that failed to mention the variable-speed centrifugal blower used to maintain air pressure, or the gasoline generator kept on stand-by in case of power failure, would arguably have omitted something of significance. After all, one of the keys to the Christos' importance is their insistence on redefining the terms in which artworks are approached and assessed. There is inevitably something absurd in this; critics of Leonardo, Rembrandt or van Gogh do not spend any more of their time than they can help on the measurements of the canvas, the composition of pigments, or the number of people it would require to hang a painting on a gallery wall. But then, these things are incidental to an understanding of art in the past, whereas the Christos, creating the esthetic climate in which their work can be understood and enjoyed, implicitly insist that statistics are essential to their projects – and in this they are routinely abetted by the critics. Comparison with rock music, and with much more in a post-modern world of art and entertainment, is inevitable: discussion of rock quickly includes production values, and subject or content have come to be considered as secondary to the impact of style.

Under the supervision of Christo, Jeanne-Claude, and their friend, chief engineer Dimiter Zagoroff, the Kassel air package was hoisted by two im-

*Lower Manhattan Wrapped Buildings,
Project for No. 2 Broadway and No. 20
Exchange Place*
Photomontage (detail from collage),
1964–1966, 52 x 75 cm
New York, Collection Horace and Holly
Solomon

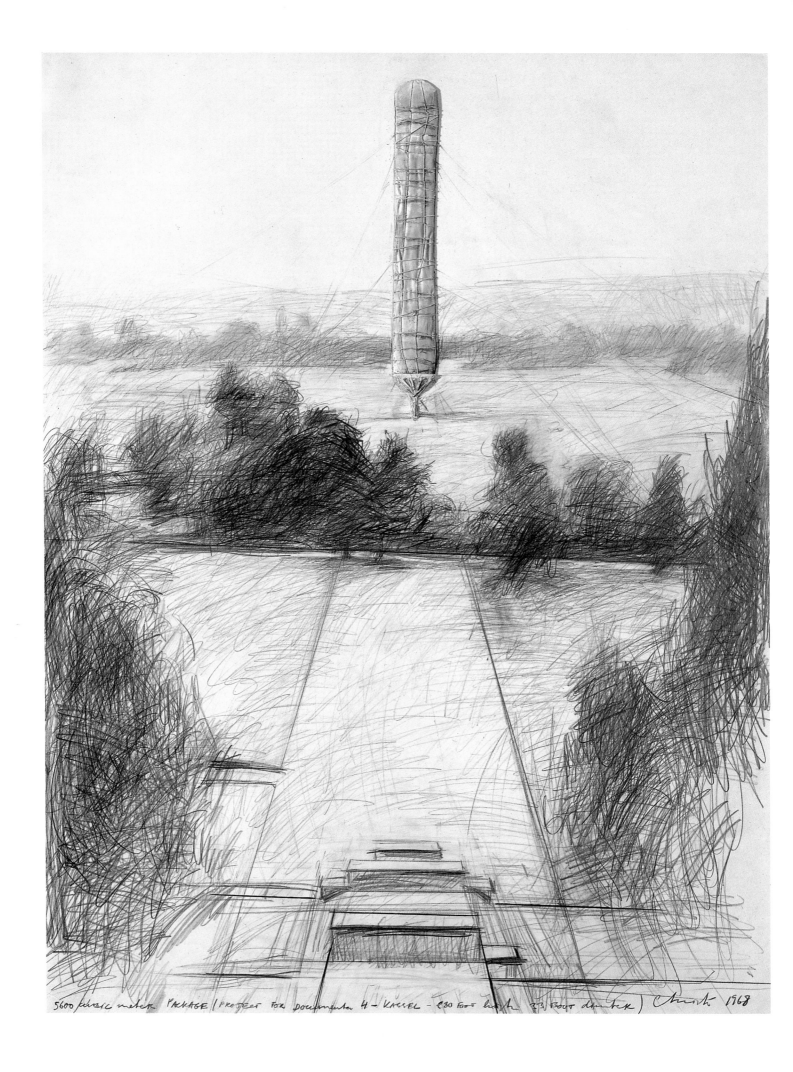

5600 *cubic meter* PACKAGE (PROJECT FOR Documenta 4 - KASSEL - 280 FOOT high 33 FOOT diameter) Christo 1968

mense cranes from its repose position into its vertical position in the air. After three unsuccessful attempts, the *Air Package* was erected (doubtless the "mot juste") between four in the morning and two in the afternoon on August 3, 1968 at that year's Kassel *documenta IV* and became one of that exhibition's most hotly discussed features (p. 35). It remained in place for two months in Karlsaue Park, in front of the Orangerie.

The Christos' work was winning an international following, especially in Europe. In 1968, in connection with the Festival of Two Worlds at the small mountain town of Spoleto in Italy, they proposed wrapping the eighteenth-century Teatro Nuovo, a three-storey opera house, but were unable to obtain the necessary permission because of fire regulations. Instead, they were permitted to wrap a 25-meter medieval tower and a baroque fountain in Spoleto's market place (p. 36). It was wrapped under the supervision of Jeanne-Claude, with the help of a team of Italian building workers, while Christo was in Germany working on the Kassel air package. The work remained in place for three weeks, throughout the Spoleto Festival, and a collaged lithograph was subsequently published.

Much of their success in persuading wary authorities to grant the necessary permissions can be traced directly to their genius for their communicating. "No artist in history," Albert Elsen has observed some years later, "has spent as much time introducing himself and his art to people around the world as Christo. The success of his projects with the public in Switzerland, West Germany, Australia, Italy, France, Japan, the United States and elsewhere is due, in no small part, to his accessibility and natural gifts as a teacher. He was the first artist to voluntarily conduct human as well as environmental impact reports for his projects. Most artists feel that having to educate the public directly takes too much time away from their own work. For Christo, verbal interaction with the public is a genuine part of his creativity."

The first European museum to be wrapped by the artists, and indeed the first building anywhere to be wrapped in its entirety, was the Kunsthalle in the Swiss capital, Berne (1968, p. 37). Their project, marking the museum's fiftieth anniversary celebrations, was one of twelve by invited environmental artists. Christo wrapped the building in 2,500 square meters of reinforced polyethylene material, and as usual securing it with some 3,000 meters of rope. Eleven workers took six days to complete the wrapping; an opening in the fabric allowed the continued use of the museum entrance throughout the week the building remained wrapped (one of the briefest projects).

A number of similar projects never came to fruition but helped confirm the growing popular perception of them as leading and innovative artists of their time. One would have involved skyscrapers on Wall Street; another, the National Gallery of Modern Art in Rome; still another, the Allied Chemical Tower (p. 1) in Times Square, (the former NY Times building). In this last case, the project proceeded as far as talks with the company, but in the end came to nothing. Two further museum wraps also fell through: first, the Whitney Museum of American Art in New York (abandoned when the well-disposed curator left the museum); and then the Museum of Modern Art in New York (p. 30). In both cases, collages and scale models were prepared, and in the event MOMA – which backed out because wrapping would have increased its insurance premium – held an exhibition of Christo's drawings, collages, and scale models for this and other projects for MOMA in June 1968.

But one further museum wrapping did come off. Visiting the Museum of Contemporary Art in Chicago to discuss a proposed exhibition of their pro-

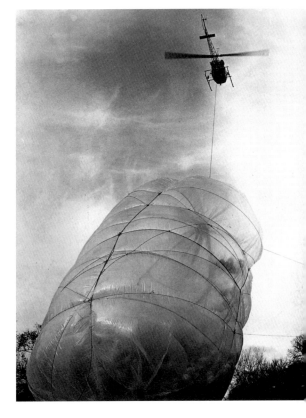

1,200 Cubic Meter Package, during elevation, 1966
Minneapolis, Minneapolis School of Art

PAGE 32:
5,600 Cubic Meter Package, Project for Kassel
Collage, 1968
Pencil, fabric and twine, 71 x 56 cm
New York, Collection Jeanne-Claude Christo

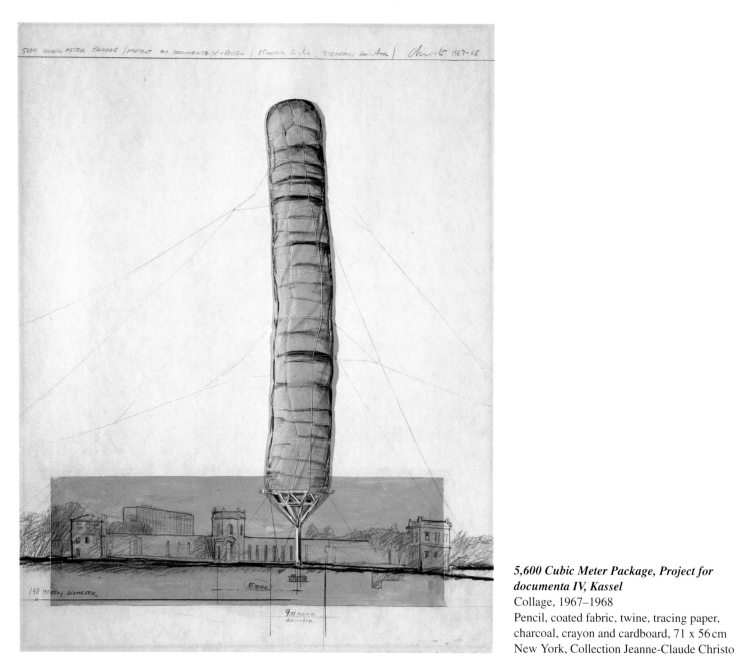

5,600 Cubic Meter Package, Project for
documenta IV, Kassel
Collage, 1967–1968
Pencil, coated fabric, twine, tracing paper,
charcoal, crayon and cardboard, 71 x 56 cm
New York, Collection Jeanne-Claude Christo

jects for wrapped buildings, the Christos were offered the opportunity to
wrap the museum by its director Jan van der Marck. "If any building ever
needed wrapping, it was Chicago's Museum of Contemporary Art," David
Bourdon later noted, "a banal, one-story edifice (with a below-ground gallery) having about as much architectural charm as a shoe-box." Wrapping
began on January 15, 1969, with students from the Art Institute of Chicago helping for two days as the building was shrouded in 1,000 square
meters of heavy tarpaulin and 1,200 meters of manila rope (pp. 38–39). All
the building's entrances and exits remained open, and small openings were
cut to keep its air vents free. The public took the result for a construction
site, and the Christos, and the Museum director were widely criticized;
Sherman E. Lee, for instance, Director of the Cleveland Museum, Ohio,
described the wrapping as a "catastrophe". The Age of '68 was of course a
period when perceived liberalism and perceived conservatism gladly went
to war over issues of esthetics, and their project doubtless provided a welcome pretext. The Chief of the Chicago Fire Department ordered the Museum to dismantle the material within forty-eight hours, but the order was

PAGE 35:
5,600 Cubic Meter Package, Kassel,
1967–1968
Coated fabric, rope, steel and air 85 x 10 m

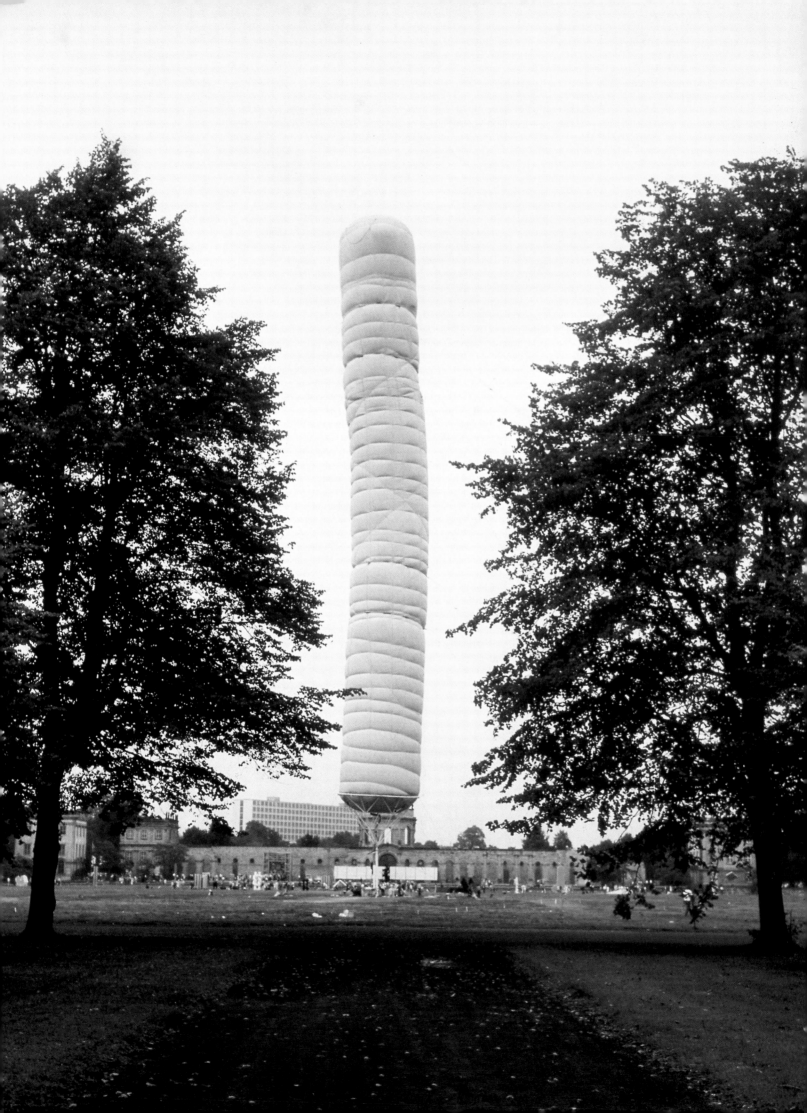

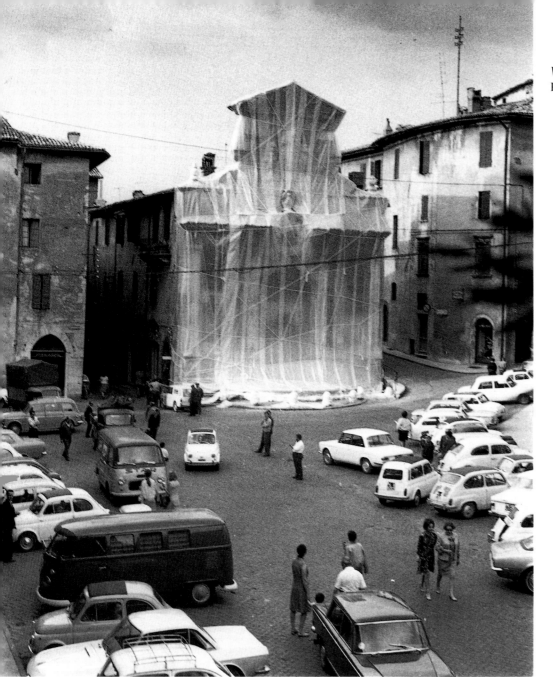

Wrapped Fountain, Spoleto, 1968
Polypropylene fabric and rope

not enforced. Meanwhile, the Christos also wrapped the 260 square meters of floor and stairway in the museum's lower gallery (cleared of paintings for the purpose), a new departure in their work (p. 39).

In 1977, Werner Spies took issue with the interpretations that were current amongst critics of the Christos in the earlier days. "Christo's shrouded museums and monuments," wrote Spies, "and his draped, blind *Store Fronts*, so it was rashly stated, spoofed our faith in wrappings, in superficialities. However, unlike the world of advertising from which Pop art took its cues, Christo shifted the focus from packaging to contents. Warhol's Soup Cans, which ironically analyze the visual facets of a unit that is barely distinguishable from others like it, lie at the other extreme: they attest to a world consisting solely of externals. By contrast, in Christo's early works the outer skin and its glossy promises are transformed into a torn veil, behind which the viewer senses content of extreme variety: museums, landscapes, monuments, life, death".

Albert Elsen, addressing the difficulties of the art-for-art's-sake position, concedes that there is "no rational purpose" for their projects, that they "do not satisfy our practical needs", and adds: "The projects are their own reason

PAGE 37 TOP:
Wrapped Kunsthalle Bern, Switzerland, 1968
Polypropylene fabric and rope

PAGE 37 BOTTOM LEFT:
Wrapped Kunsthalle Bern, Switzerland, 1968
Polypropylene, fabric and rope

PAGE 37 BOTTOM RIGHT:
Wrapped Kunsthalle Bern, Switzerland, Project for the Fiftieth Anniversary of the Kunsthalle
Collage, 1968
Pencil, fabric, twine, photograph by Harry Shunk, charcoal and crayon, 71 x 56 cm
Collection The Lilja Art Fund Foundation

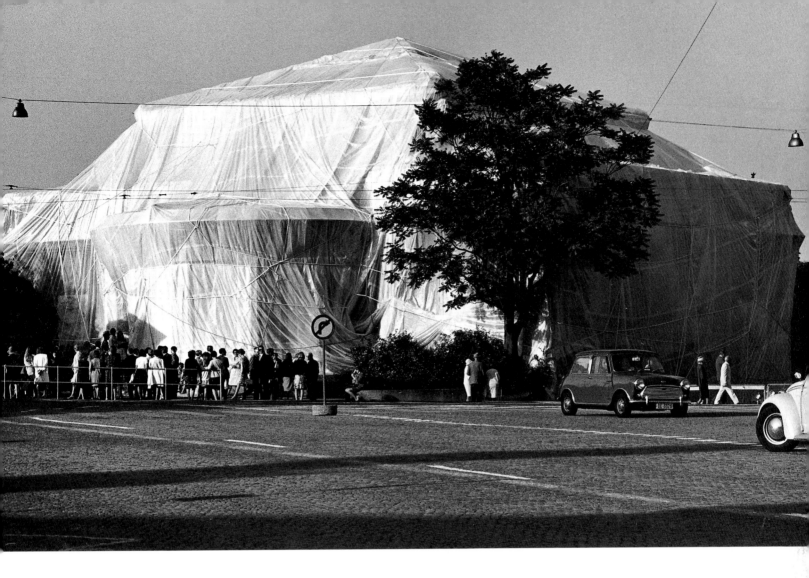

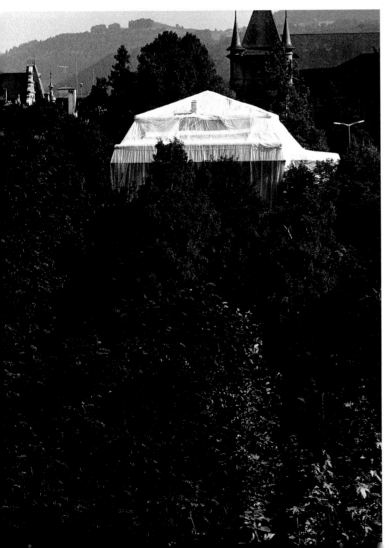

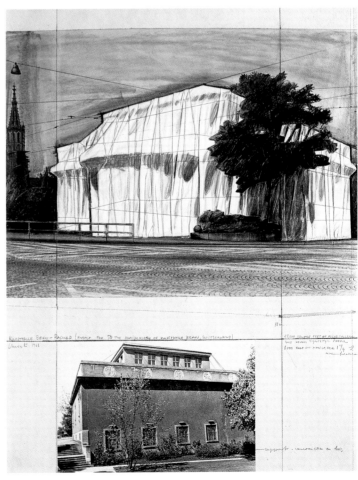

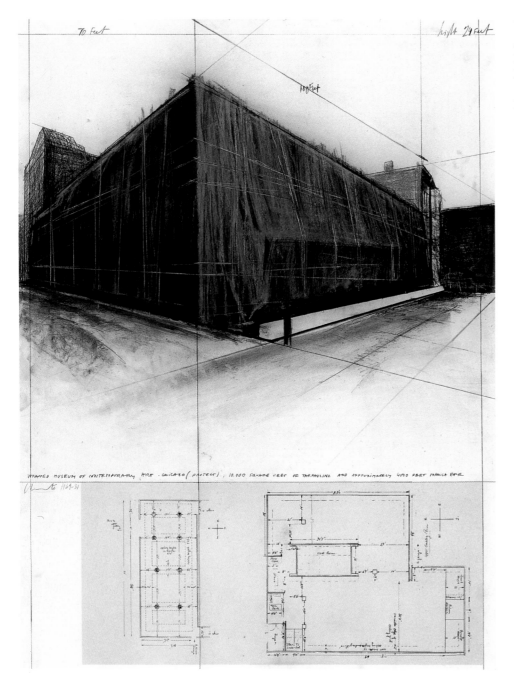

Wrapped Museum of Contemporary Art,
Project for Chicago
Drawing-collage, 1969–1981
Pencil, charcoal, crayon and tracing paper
107 x 83 cm
New York, Collection Jeanne-Claude Christo

for being" – which might serve as the definition of art for art's sake. But Elsen goes on (and this is significant): "In the late twentieth century they are also tributes to artistic freedom. Christo confronts what does exist with what he alone has determined can exist as a dramatic and beautiful form. His art therefore is the result of intelligence and esthetic intuition added to the natural and built environment."

And Elsen concludes, in words that the present writer and many thousands of others can confirm: "We often understand all this only when we have experienced the projects directly and realized that in a poetic way our lives have been changed, as has our comprehension of what art can be and do." We all know Rilke's sonnet in which the poet stands before a statue of Apollo and feels the imperative of true art: "You must change your life." In some sense, the Christos' art is telling us the same.

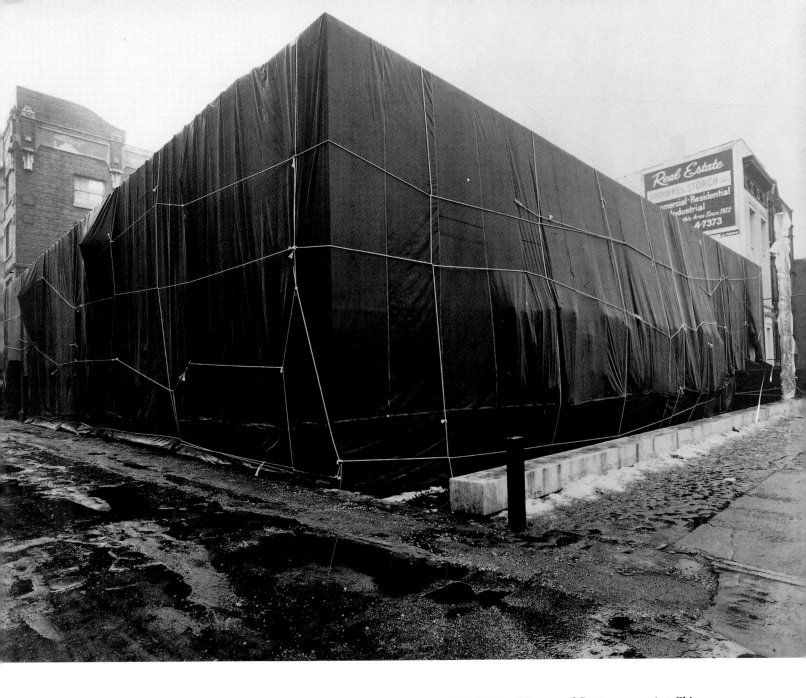

Museum of Contemporary Art, Chicago, Wrapped, 1969
Tarpaulin fabric and rope

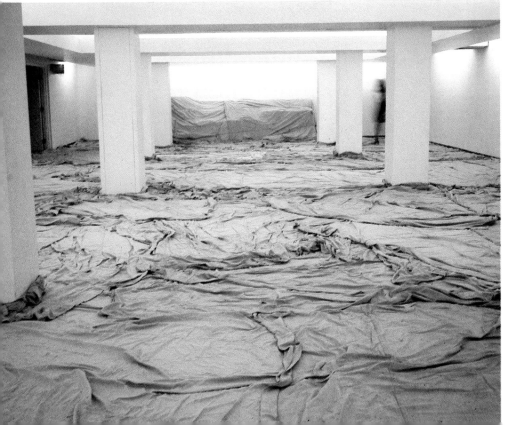

Wrapped Floor and Stairway, Museum of Contemporary Art, Chicago, 1969
Cotton drop cloth and rope

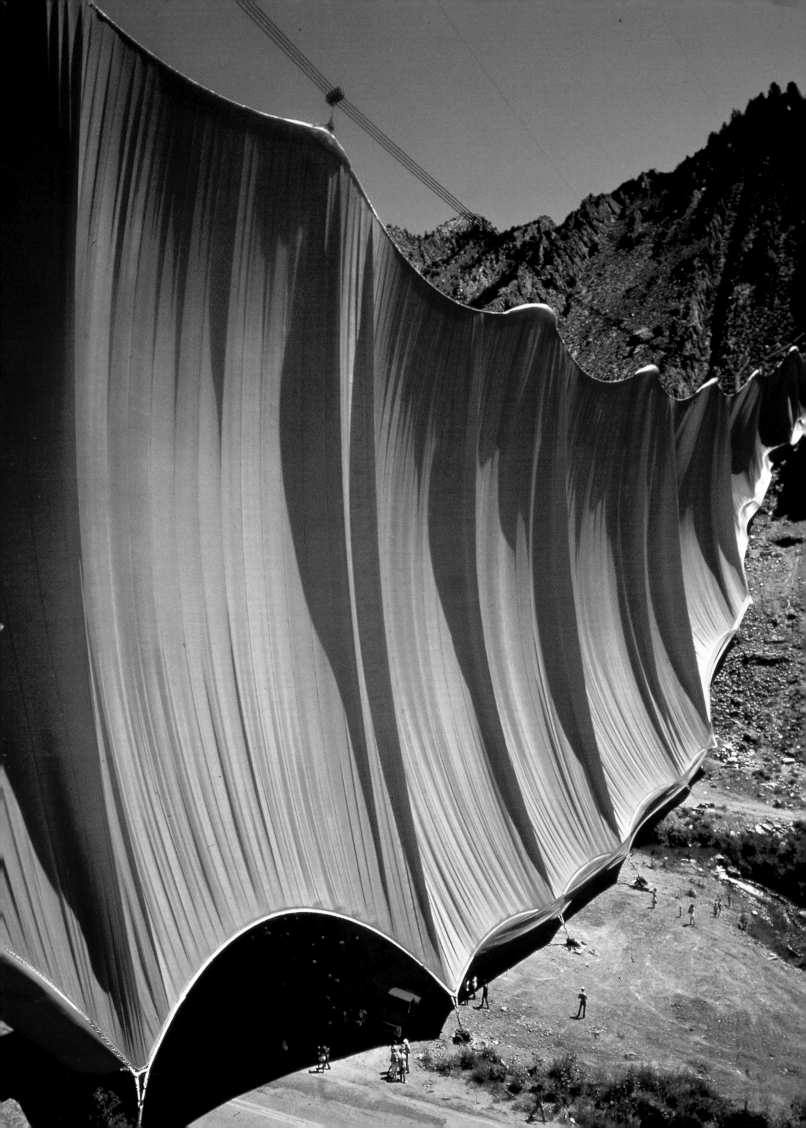

"The quintessential artist of his time"
Wrapped Coast, Valley Curtain, Running Fence

"Christo accomplishes three things at once," British art critic Marina Vaizey has observed. "He makes things of uncanny beauty that exist for a while in the real world. Christo's are art: artificial, constructed, man-made. Christo's enhance the real world, sharpen our vision, make us more aware and observant, and finally, change the way we see things. He is particularly acute about boundaries: about fences, paths, bridges, where in the real world things change, the land becomes coastline and beach, bridges arch over water. And he uses the materials of the contemporary world, the oil-based product of plastics, fabrics of nylon, of woven polypropylene, of concrete, of steel cables and steel poles. [...] Christo is the quintessential artist of his time, and our time."

Vaizey's statement may seem extravagant at first glance, but it repays careful consideration. "It is the age of information, and of propaganda, of advertising, packaging, presentation and wrapping," Vaizey reminds us. "We are inundated with images as never before." And in this brave new world, ancient longings familiarly surface among the people in it: "It is an age of mass production and of a longing for nature, the natural, the individual, the handmade. In the late twentieth century, people are acutely aware of an astonishing melange of contradictory hopes, dreams and desires, of many realities. And art is not only the physical embodiment of aspirations and faith, the way in which we can explain the world to ourselves, make patterns by which to grasp the unimaginable and incomprehensible, but also a commodity and a currency."

Against this background, they can be seen as the very personification of the contrarieties, aspirations, stresses and capabilities of art in the modern world. "Christo," declares Vaizey, "is the artist who inimitably has come to combine in his art the force of the individual creator with the methods of industrial and post-industrial society: capitalism, democracy, enquiry, experiment, collaboration and co-operation. In the course of so doing, Christo has moved from eastern Europe, from Bulgaria, to a Europe that was temporarily neutral, to Austria, to France and Paris, the traditional capital of the avant-garde, and finally to New York, the post-war art capital, the essential consumerist, capitalist city." Both in its shape and in its implications, the Christos' career has offered the definitive map of art in today's society.

In the decade from the late 1960s to late 1970s, the Christos created some of their most startlingly beautiful works in natural environments. The first, one of their greatest triumphs, came about when John Kaldor, a Sydney textiles businessman, invited the Christos to Australia to exhibit and lecture. The invitation coincided with their need for a site where they could realize a project to wrap a stretch of coastline, and the result was the *Wrapped Coast* (1968–1969, pp. 42–43) – 100,000 square meters of wrapped coast at Little

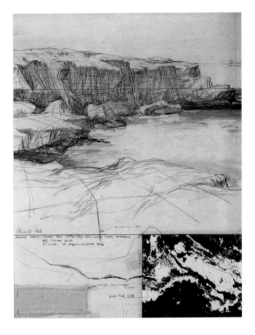

Wrapped Coast, Project for Little Bay, Australia
Drawing collage, 1969
Pencil, crayon, aerial photograph, tape and woven polypropylene fabric sample, 71 x 56 cm
Private Collection

PAGE 40:
Valley Curtain, Rifle, Colorado, 1970–1972
Nylon polyamide, steel cables, rope and concrete, 111 x 381 m

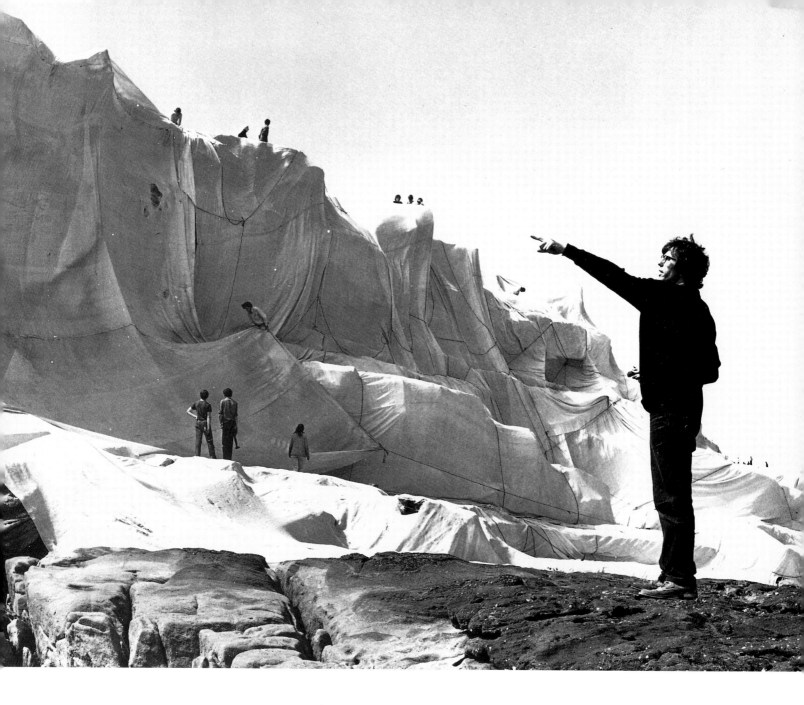

Christo at the *Wrapped Coast, Little Bay,
Australia, 1969*

Bay, Sydney. To this day, the Christos' name has remained synonymous with that project in Australia: it was "a watershed for contemporary art in Australia," as Kaldor later observed, and "did more for contemporary art in Australia than any other single event," as Edmund Capon, Director of the Art Gallery of New South Wales, Sydney, put it.

Little Bay is about 14 kilometers south-east of Sydney. The craggy shoreline stretch that was wrapped was about 2.4 kilometers long, up to 250 meters wide, and ranged from sea level at the sandy beach to a height of 26 meters at the northern cliffs.

100,000 square meters of erosion-control fabric (synthetic woven fibre, usually manufactured for agricultural purposes) were used for the wrapping and 56 kilometers of polypropylene rope three centimeters in diameter tied the fabric to the rocks.

A team of 15 professional mountain climbers, 110 laborers, and students of art and architecture from the University of Sydney and the East Sydney Technical College, toiled for some 17,000 man-hours, joined by a number of Australian artists and teachers eager to lend a helping hand. The expenses were met by the Christos from the sale of original preparatory drawings and collages (cf. p.41).

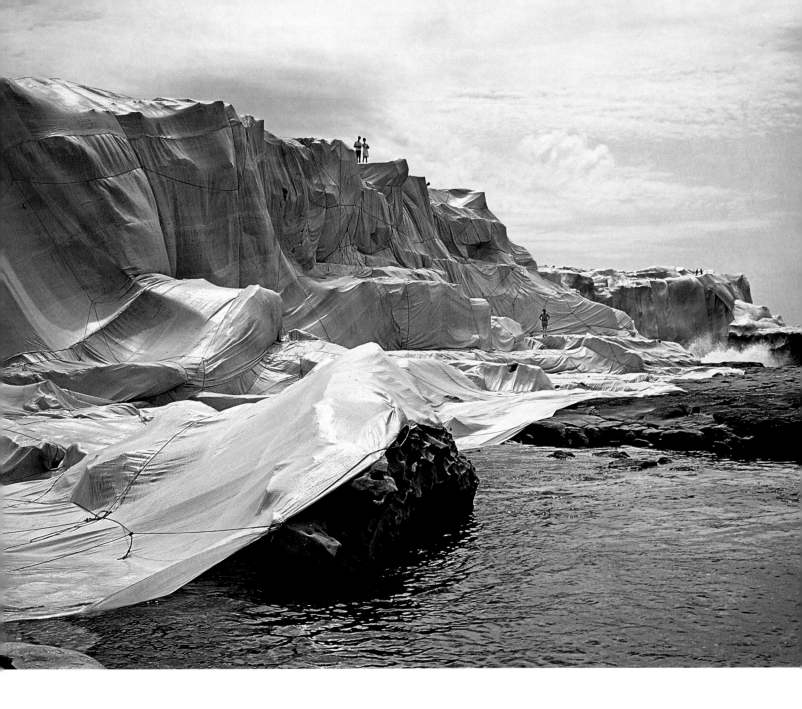

It is worth emphasizing that after the ten-week period for which the coastal stretch was wrapped (from October to December 1969) the materials were removed and the site (which many thousands had visited) returned to its original state.

Landscape or environmental art of the Christos' kind has no exact parallels, but it is striking that comparable art – art that makes use of available natural landscape – does not always respect the environment as scrupulously. The famous Blue Mountains north of Mount Sinai, for instance, are a breathtaking example of land art created in two months in 1980 by Belgian artist Jean Vérame, using only paint and brushes. Beautiful as this painted rocky landscape in a remote region is, though, it bears the artist's imprint permanently: the landscape cannot be returned to its natural condition (as it can after the Christos have completed a project).

"Christo's art," wrote Albert Elsen in a 1990 Sydney exhibition catalog, "is the creation of temporary, beautiful objects on a vast scale for specific outdoor sites. It is in the populist nature of his thinking that he believes people should have intense and memorable experiences of art outside museums." Or, as Jeanne-Claude put it to the present writer, "Each one of our works is a scream of freedom". As the 1970s began, the Christos con-

Wrapped Coast, Little Bay, Australia,
1968–1969 (detail)
Polypropylene fabric and rope, 250 x 2,400 m

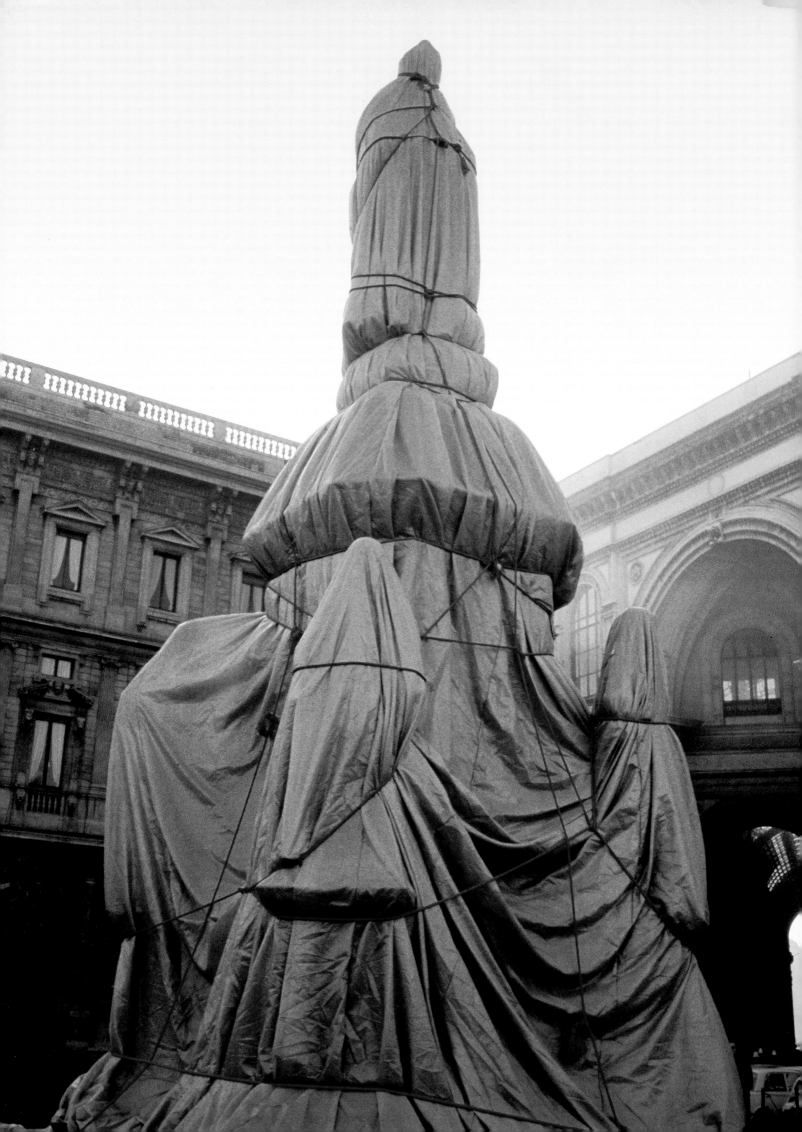

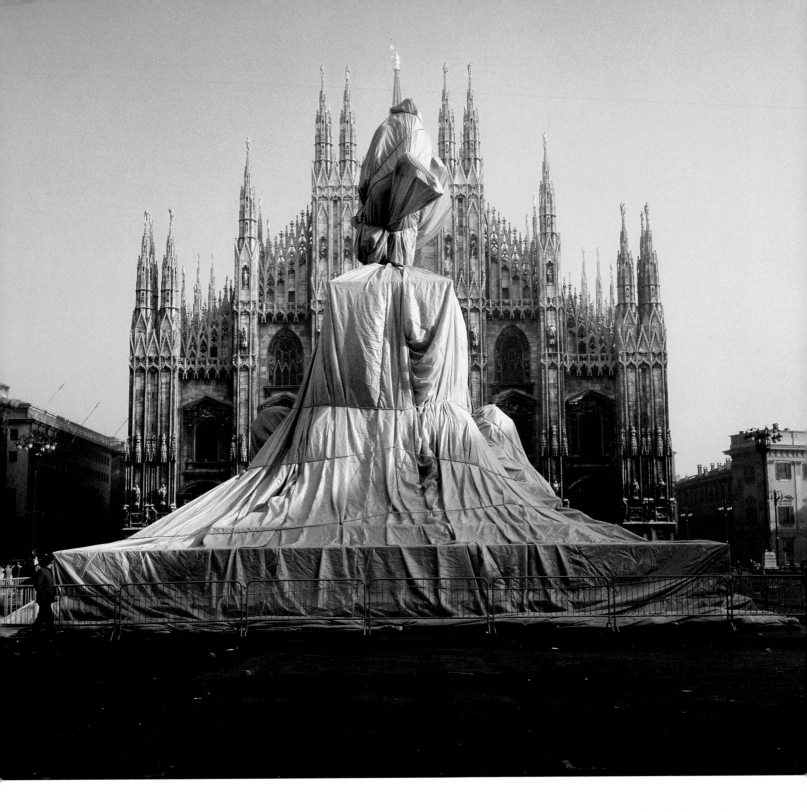

ceived a number of projects on a smaller scale before going on to the *Valley Curtain*, and one of these is particularly worth mentioning. In 1970 the city of Milan organized a major exhibition to mark the tenth anniversary of the founding of the *Nouveaux Réalistes*. For that the Christos devised two temporary projects.

One was the wrapping of the monument to Leonardo da Vinci (1970, p. 44), which remained enveloped in white fabric and rope on the Piazza della Scala for several days; the other was the wrapping of the monument to Vittorio Emanuele, the last King of Italy (1970, p. 45). This imposing statue, in front of the Duomo in Milan, remained wrapped for forty-eight hours. The Milanese wrappings brought the issue of dignity (and its arguable infringement) to a head for the first time as the cases for and against were thrashed out.

Wrapped Monument to Vittorio Emanuele, Piazza del Duomo, Milan, 1970
Polypropylene fabric and rope

PAGE 44:
Wrapped Monument to Leonardo, Piazza della Scala, Milan, 1970
Polypropylene fabric and rope

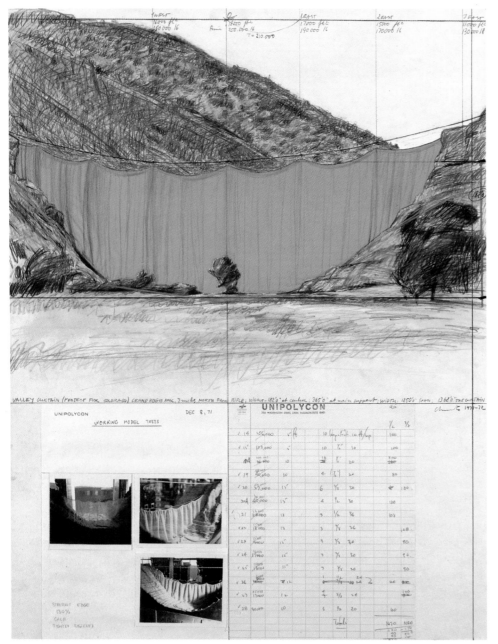

Valley Curtain, Project for Rifle, Colorado
Collage, 1971–1972
Pencil, fabric, pastel, three photographs by
Dimiter Zagoroff, charcoal, crayon, ballpoint
pen and technical data, 71 x 56 cm
New York, Collection Jeanne-Claude Christo

The next significant outdoor project after the Australian coast near
Sydney was the *Valley Curtain* at Rifle, Colorado (1970–72, p. 40, p. 47),
planning for which had begun in 1970. At 11 a.m. on August 10, 1972 at
Rifle (between Grand Junction and Glenwood Springs in the Grand Hog-
back Mountain Range), a group of 35 construction workers and 64 temporary helpers, art school and college students, and itinerant workers, tied down
the last of 27 ropes that secured the 13,000 square meters of woven nylon
fabric orange curtain to its moorings at Rifle Gap, 11 kilometers north of
Rifle, on Highway 325.

The curtain measured 381 meters in width and up to 111 meters in height,
and remained clear of the slopes and the valley floor. The cables holding it
in place spanned 417 meters, weighed fifty tons, and were anchored to 800
tons of concrete foundations.

So much hard work! And so much time (28 months in all) in the making!
And the following day, August 11, a gale swept through the valley at a speed
of 100 kilometers per hour, and made it necessary to begin removal: the
temporary nature of the Christos' works was being driven home by the ele-

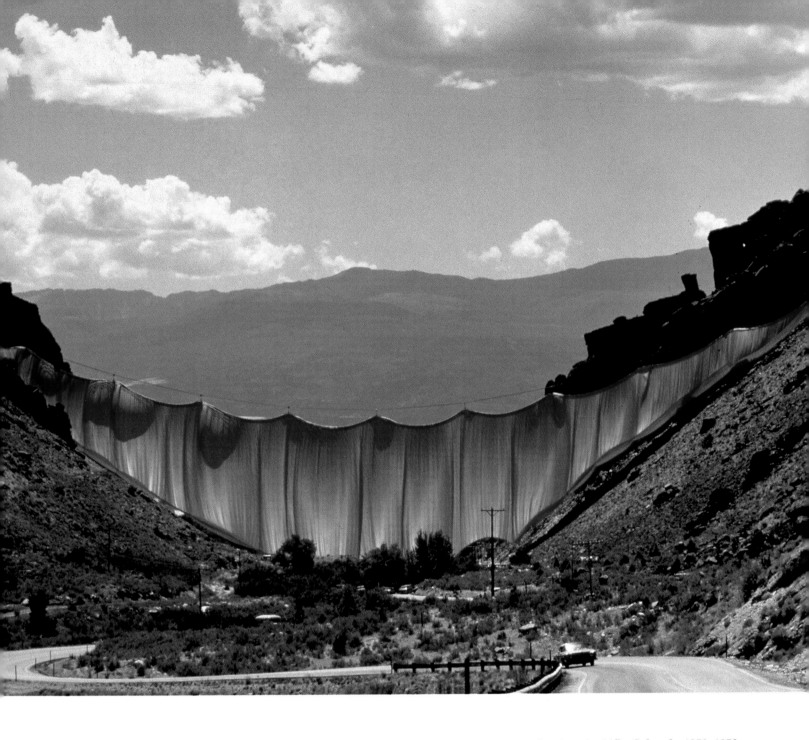

ments. "He momentarily intervenes," as Albert Elsen has aptly put it, "creating 'gentle disturbances' between earth and sky in order to refocus our
impressions […] Christo believes the temporary nature of his projects gives
them more energy and intensifies our response. But once he has wrapped a
structure or intervened in a place, he is forever associated with that site."
Again and again, temporariness becomes the issue – and arguably a more
pertinent issue than the somewhat airy "forever" invoked by Elsen, which
would be a "forever" wholly bounded by human lifespans if there were no
other witness to the Christos' projects than the memories of those who were
there. "After the work has been prepared, and after the work has been put up
and then taken down, it remains" asserts Marina Vaizey. "It remains in the
memory of the thousands who will have experienced it first hand; it remains
in the memory of those who will have seen the work on film, on television,
in the newspapers. And an integral part is Christo's own portable art, the
magnificent sketches, drawings, collages and prints that are both his working drawings and works of art in their own right." Memory is limited in
time, but the accompanying and preparatory works Christo makes in the

Valley Curtain, Rifle, Colorado, 1970–1972
Nylon polyamide, steel cable, rope and
concrete, 111 x 381 m

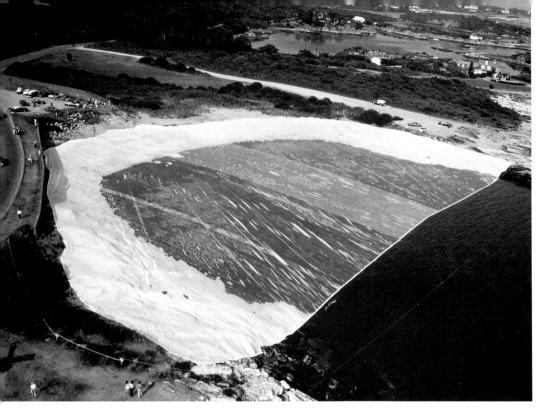

course of the projects palpably have the age-old function of defying time
and insisting that they (and thus the artwork as a whole) will endure. The argument involving the memories of those who see their artworks, so often
put forward, has precarious implications, since it can lead us to conclude
that art need exist only in the mind – a fallacy, surely. But Christo's ancillary
works do indeed have the function of declaring that his creations remain.
Given the artists' own insistence on temporariness, there may well be a para-
dox hidden here, and one not easily resolved.

Before their next major landscape project, the Christos returned to the
urban setting once more (town and country have alternated throughout their
career) for the *The Wall – Wrapped Roman Wall* work (1974, p.49). The
wall in question was at the end of the Via Veneto, one of Rome's busiest
thoroughfares, near the gardens of the Villa Borghese. Two thousand years
old, it was built under the Emperor Marcus Aurelius. Christo and Jeanne-
Claude wrapped a length of over 259 meters in polypropylene fabric and
rope; and, for the duration of forty wrapped days, three of the four wrapped
arches continued to be used by traffic and the fourth by pedestrians. The response in Rome was a lively one.

That same year, the Christos created the *Ocean Front* (1974, p.48) at Newport, Rhode Island. For eighteen days, 14,000 square meters of white woven
polypropylene fabric covered the surface of the water of a cove shaped like a
half-moon at King's Beach, on the southern exposure of Ocean Drive, facing
that portion of the Long Island Sound that meets the Atlantic at Rhode Island.
As with the *Valley Curtain* project, Mitko Zagoroff, John Thomson and Jim
Fuller were the engineers who designed and supervised the construction
itself. "Work began," ran the Christos' official bulletin, "at 6.00 a.m. on Mon-
day, August 19, 1974. The bundled fabric was passed from the truck to pairs
of non-skilled workers wearing life-jackets. They carried the 2,722 kilograms
of fabric to the water on two-by-fours stretched between them. The fabric
was laced to a wooden boom 120 meters long, secured with twelve Danforth
anchors, holding in place the frontal edge of the floating fabric".

These communiqués have become an integral part of the Christos' projects over the years. Their promotional and communicative skills have been
widely attested, and Marina Vaizey has gone so far as to claim that "the

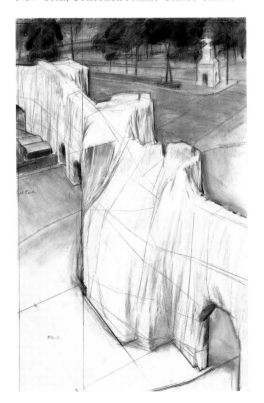

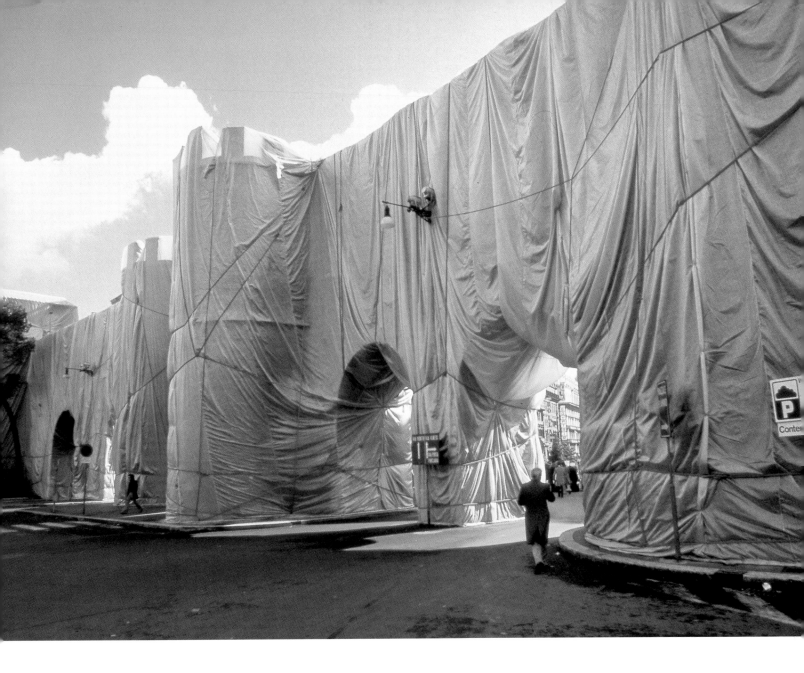

The Wall – Wrapped Roman Wall, Rome,
1974
Polypropylene fabric and rope, 15 x 259 m

Christo presentation, the Christo interview, is itself a piece of Christo art".
More level-headed, perhaps, is her observation that "Christo has evolved
ways of involving society in the making of his art". That, surely, is the prime
implication of the famous bulletins, the media manipulations, the public
persona; though some see them as narcissistic or even megalomaniac, the
point is in reality a quite different one: he and Jeanne-Claude want their
ideas and proposals out in the public arena, where they can be inspected, debated and considered from every angle, in a fashion that is more profoundly
democratic in implication than the approaches taken by many another self-
proclaimed egalitarian in art.

Arguably the loveliest and most spectacular of the Christos' epic projects was the *Running Fence* (1972–1976, p. 51), 39.5 kilometers long, in
Sonoma and Marin Counties north of San Francisco. Against considerable
opposition, the Christos won through and put up their long white fence
stretching in from the Pacific Ocean, across farms, past villages. To reach
that point, they had gone through 18 public hearings and three sessions at
the superior courts of California, and had drawn up an environmental impact report the size of a telephone directory. It was the first E.I.R. ever
done on a work of art. But the reward was visible to all. The beauty of the
snaking fence was enhanced by its oblique similarity to the Great Wall of

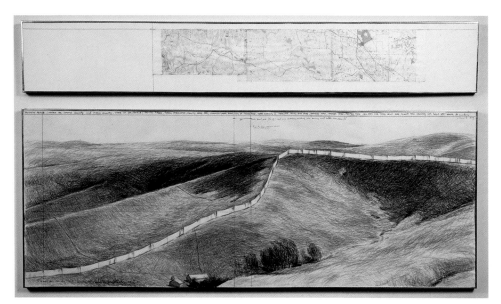

Running Fence, Project for Sonoma and Marin Counties, California
Drawing, 1973, in two parts
Pencil, crayon and topographic map, in two parts: 35.5 x 244 and 91.5 x 244 cm
New York, Collection Jeanne-Claude Christo

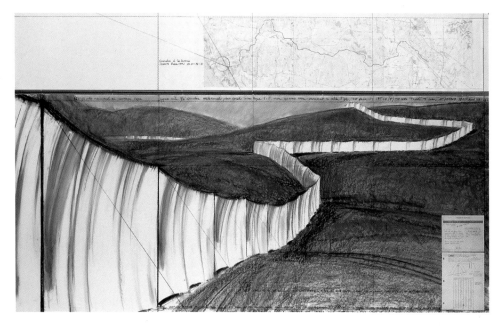

Running Fence, Project for Sonoma and Marin Counties, California
Drawing, 1976, in two parts:
Pastel, pencil and charcoal, crayon, technical data and map, 38 x 244 and 106.6 x 244 cm
New York, Collection Jeanne-Claude Christo
Running Fence, Sonoma and Marin Counties, California, 1972–1976
Nylon fabric, poles and steel cables, 5.5 m x 39.5 km

China; and that similarity was eerily underpinned by the coincidental fact that Chairman Mao Tse-Tung died on the day before the *Running Fence* was completed. Coincidences are not germane to a work of art, but they can unwittingly heighten its impact.

The *Running Fence*, 5.5 meters high and 39.5 kilometers long, extending across the properties of fifty-nine ranchers near Freeway 101 north of San Francisco, following the rolling hills and dropping down to the Pacific at Bodega Bay, was completed on September 10, 1976. All the white nylon fabric (160,000 square meters), the steel cables (145 kilometers) and poles (2,060), and the earth anchors (14,000), were designed for complete removal: no visible evidence remained on the hills of Sonoma and Marin Counties to indicate that the *Running Fence* had ever been there. The removal began (as agreed with the ranchers and the authorities) fourteen days after completion.

"He borrows land, public structures and spaces," Albert Elsen wrote. "Unlike a warrior-ruler such as Napoleon, who is forever associated with sites by force of arms, Christo's permanent identification with places and historic structures is by the force of art." On the matter of permanence, opinion is

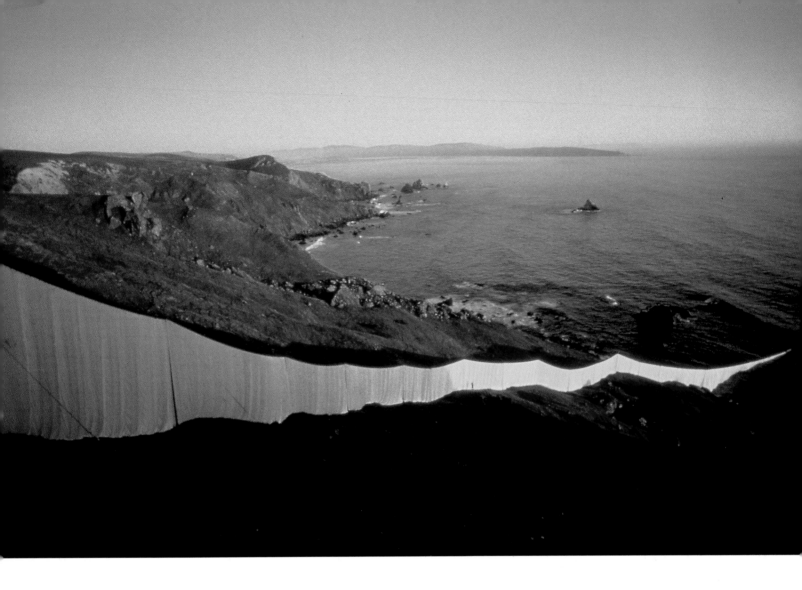

naturally still divided – not least because it is obviously too early to say; in any case, the Christos themselves would be the first to object to the introduction of the idea of permanence into art projects defined by their temporary nature. But the artists' identification with their sites can be confirmed by anyone who drove the 65 kilometers of public roads in Sonoma and Marin Counties from which the *Running Fence* was meant to be viewed. The excited international response to the work reflected a simple truth: that the Christos, in impressing their own intuition of beauty upon the landscape, were expressing intuitions shared by many.

The *Wrapped Walk Ways* (1978, p.55) that followed (in Kansas City's Jacob L. Loose Park) were like chamber music after a grand symphony in the Romantic tradition, but they possessed their own intimate beauty. To prepare the 12,540 square meters of saffron nylon fabric, an army of seamstresses at a West Virginia factory and on site in the park were employed, and a task force of 84 people was needed to install the material. Over four kilometers of walkways in formal gardens and jogging paths, remained covered from October 4 to 16, 1978, after which the material was removed and given to the Kansas City Parks Department for recycling, and the park itself restored to its original condition.

The project was popular with the public: as so often, part of the Christos' charismatic success derived from their ability to mobilize large numbers of people, inculcating a team spirit and a joint sense of achievement. In this respect, their orchestrated projects were compared by some critics with theatrical or musical enterprises. Marina Vaizey reminds us that the co-operative approach has time-honoured roots in artistic tradition: "We are used to the

Running Fence, Sonoma and Marin Counties, California, 1972–1976
Nylon fabric, poles and steel cables, 5.5 m x 39.5 km

In order to obtain the necessary permits from the governmental agencies in California, the artists had to prepare a 355-page environmental impact report, 1972–1976

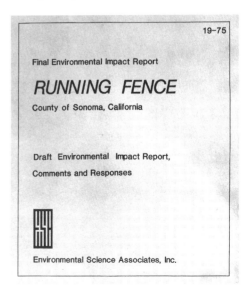

19–75

Final Environmental Impact Report

RUNNING FENCE

County of Sonoma, California

Draft Environmental Impact Report,

Comments and Responses

Environmental Science Associates, Inc.

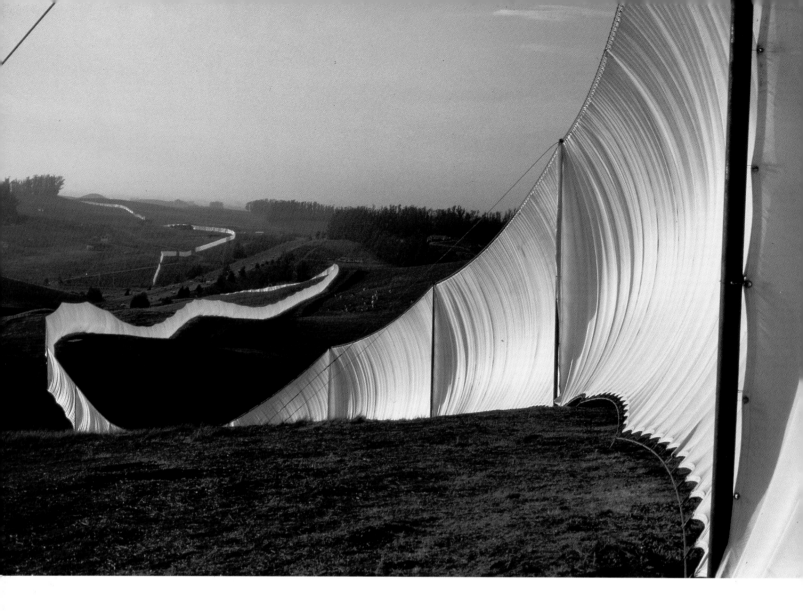

Running Fence, Sonoma and Marin Counties, California, 1972–1976
Nylon fabric, poles and steel cables,
5.5 m x 39.5 km

PAGE 53:

Running Fence, Sonoma and Marin Counties, California, 1972–1976
Nylon fabric, poles and steel cables,
5.5 m x 39.5 km

notion of collaborative projects in art and technology in two different ways. In both art and design there is the notion of the studio, of apprentices, students, assistants, and specialists working under artistic direction. This is a practice well-established in the early Renaissance, and which evolved from the ways in which craftsmen and artists were once indistinguishable philosophically, although each individual might have a speciality. For example, in northern Italy in the fourteenth century, the creation of devotional works of art required several skills, not necessarily all practised by the same person. Some prepared the panels, some were specialist gilders, some painters, and the person to whom the panel was ascribed was in charge of the overall design and composition, although he would not have made it entirely on his own."

"He has harnessed the methods of democratic capitalism to the making of art," Marina Vaizey has observed. "His method is inseparable from his art [...] He and his work are at home in the centre of cities, and in remote countryside. He has made huge projects that have existed for only days or weeks, then to vanish forever, memorialized only by the media, and in the memories of those hundreds of people involved in the process of their making." The immortality of artworks, inscribed over the centuries into our consciousness of sculpted stone or printed page or long-surviving melody, has never been more radically defied than by the Christos' works – often involving elaborate technical operations, months or years of planning, and the labor of many, only to disappear, leaving no trace at the site where they were created.

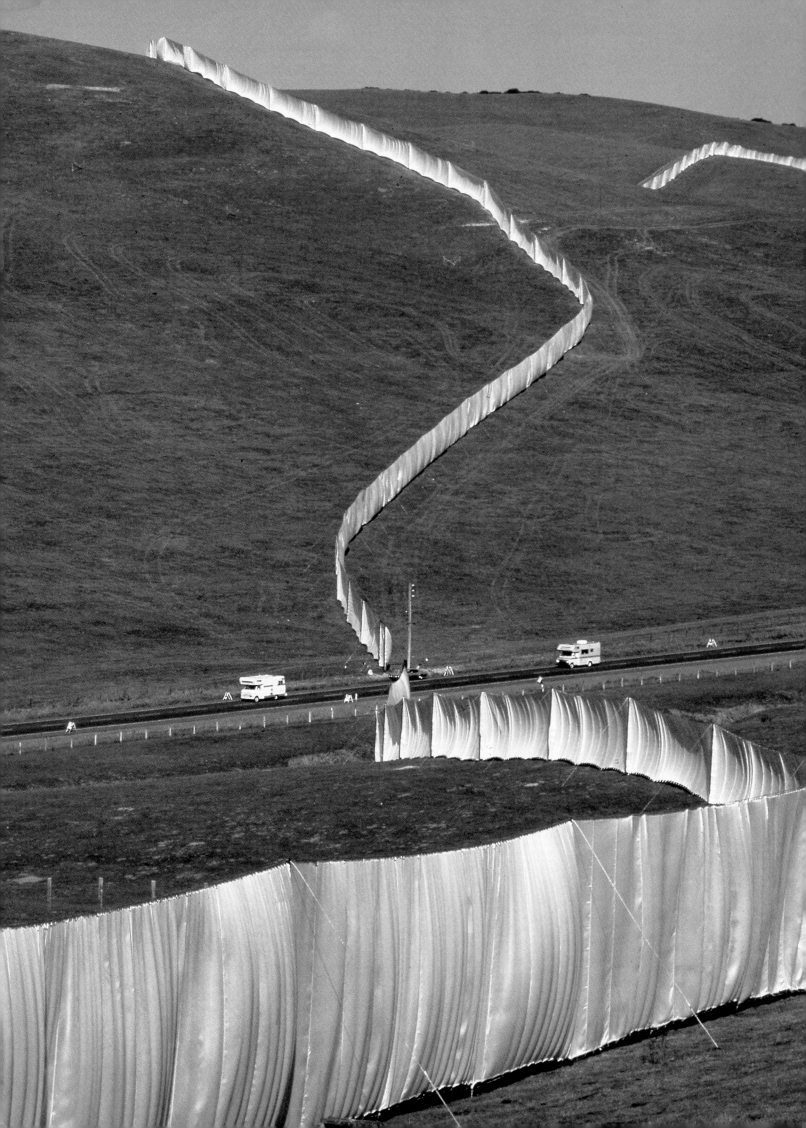

PAGE 55:

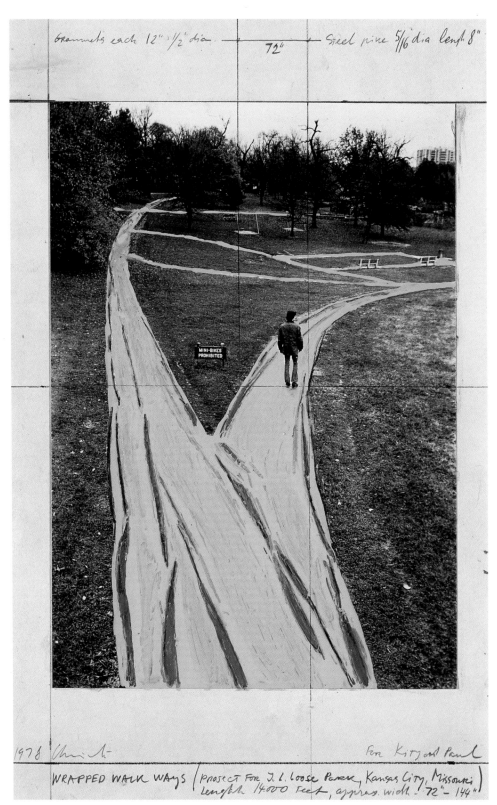

Wrapped Walk Ways, Jacob L. Loose Park,
Kansas City, Missouri, 1977–1978
Fabric covering 4.5 km of walkways

Wrapped Walk Ways, Project for Jacob L.
Loose Park, Kansas City, Missouri
Collage, 1978
Pencil, enamel paint, photograph by Wolfgang
Volz, crayon and charcoal, 38 x 28 cm
New York, Collection Jeanne-Claude Christo

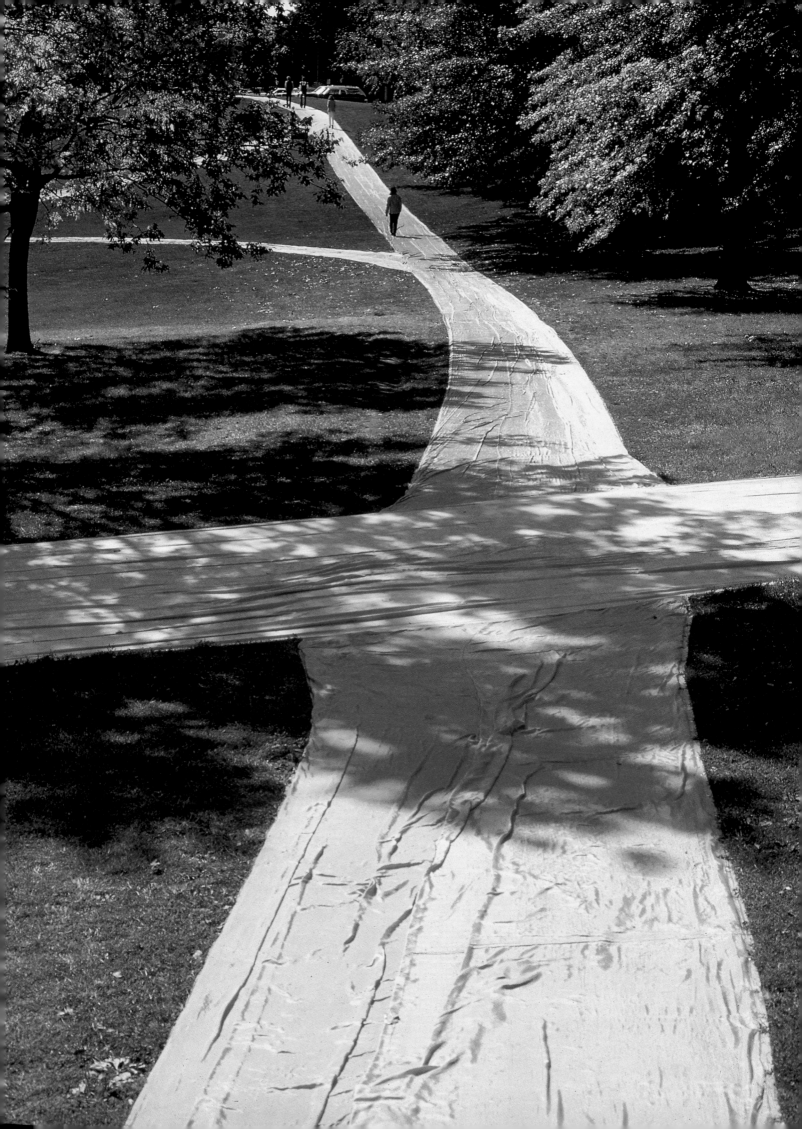

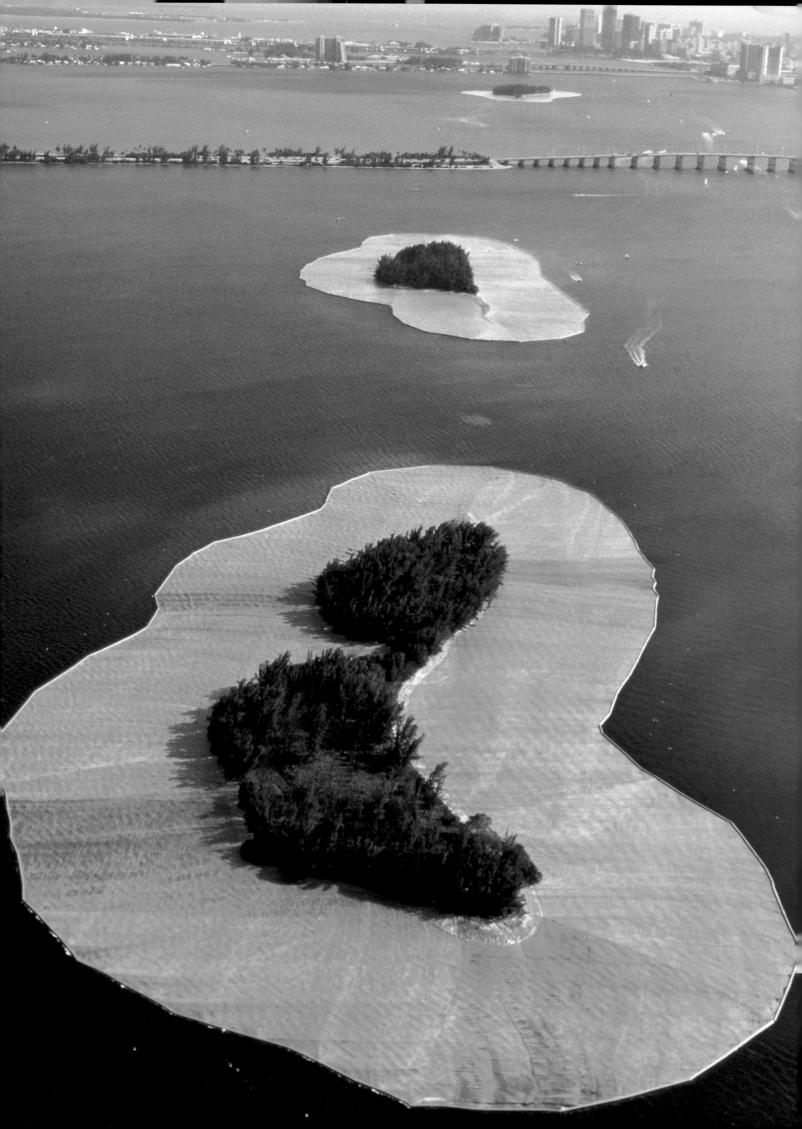

"The only natural choice"
Surrounded Islands, Pont-Neuf, The Umbrellas

One of the most spectacular projects conceived and created by the Christos, a personal favorite of the present writer, was the *Surrounded Islands* (1980–1983, p.56) in Biscayne Bay, Greater Miami, Florida. This mammoth project – accommodated to the natural environment, symbiotically blending with it without harm or disturbance – was a work of great beauty, delicacy and poetry, as well as daring, and posed considerable risk and technical difficulty.

In a project they saw as an urban enterprise, the Christos set out to surround eleven man-made islands set squarely amidst the millions that populate Greater Miami, islands that were used mostly for dumping garbage. The preparations were long and complex, and involved, as in other projects, drawings, collages and photographs, as well as documentation and numerous meetings with government and local officials, in order to secure permissions. From April 1981, a team of attorneys, a marine engineer, four consulting engineers and a building contractor, a marine biologist, an ornithologist, and an expert on mammals, all worked steadily on preparing the *Surrounded Islands Project*. Marine and land crews picked up debris from the eleven islands, putting refuse in bags and removing some 40 tons of rubbish in all. Permits were obtained from the Governor of Florida, the City of Miami Commission, and numerous other authorities, including the U.S. Army Corps of Engineers: "The US Army Corps of Engineers permit alone is six inches thick," reported the *Miami Herald*, "thicker than a Bible, thicker than the Websters Third International Dictionary unabridged edition." And the result was one of the most unforgettable and poetic sights art has produced in modern times.

I well remember taking a helicopter and flying over the islands. The panorama that was revealed before us showed yet again how precious was the Christos' gift for transformation. The landscape *per se* had been metamorphosed, for a short time, into another, beautiful reality, with luminous pink surrounds of fabric shining in breathtakingly unusual harmony with the tropical vegetation of the islands, the light of the Miami sky, and the colors of the shallow waters of the bay. Claude Monet's *Water Lilies* (1916, p.60) inevitably came to mind; the islands seemed to be floating pads of verdure and blossom, observed (rather than made) by an eye sensitive to every nuance of light and color.

The choice of pink fabric was far from accidental. "Pink, with the sweetish overtones of frangipani, will strike the stranger to Miami within a matter of hours as the symbolic color of the area," observed Werner Spies. "Pink was the only natural choice of color in that part of the country – the color of a euphoric artificiality." In the Christos' use of the color, there was both humor and affection. And the color did not go unglossed by the press. "In Miami," noted *The Orlando Sentinel* (April 17, 1983), "pink used to mean flamingos, sunsets and art deco hotels. Now it means Christo."

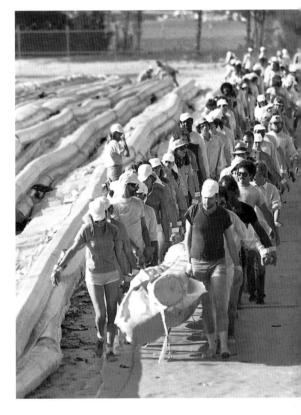

Surrounded Islands, Biscayne Bay, Greater Miami, Florida, during installation, May 1983

PAGE 56:
Surrounded Islands, Biscayne Bay, Greater Miami, Florida, 1983
603,850 square meters of fabric floating around 11 islands

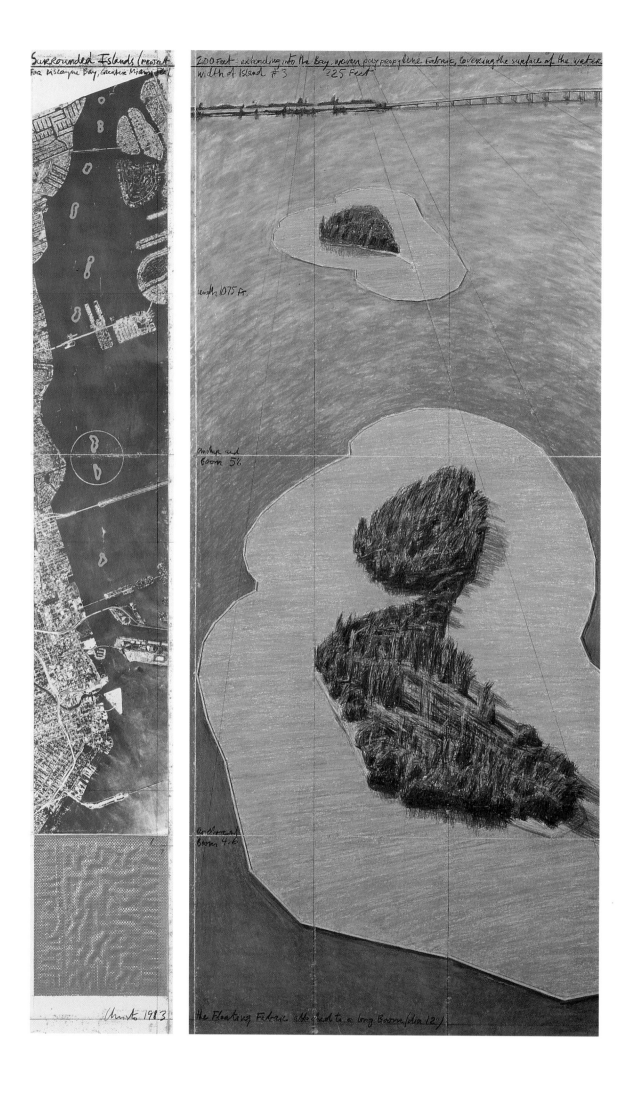

Surrounded Islands (project
For Biscayne Bay, Greater Miami, Fla.)

200 Feet - extending into the Bay, woven polypropylene fabric, covering the surface of the water
width of Island #3   325 Feet

length 1075 ft.

anchor and
boom 5'6

length 1075 ft.

Anchor and
Boom 4.6

Christo 1983

the Floating Fabric attached to a long Boom (dia 12")

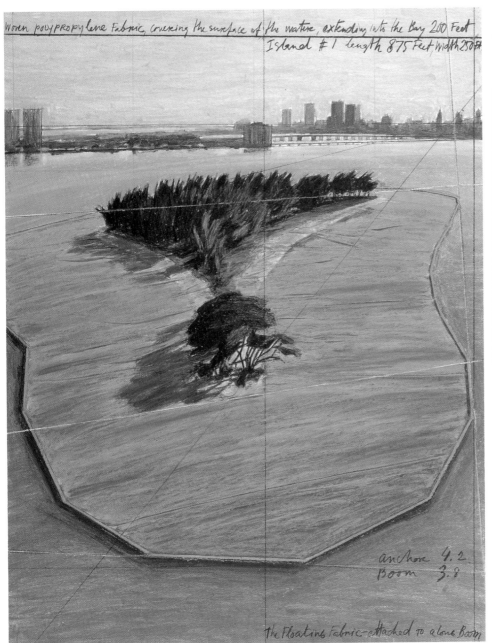

Handwritten annotations on image:
woven polypropylene fabric, covering the surface of the water, extending into the Bay 200 Feet
Island #1 length 875 Feet / Width 250 ft
anchor 4.2
Boom 3.8
The Floating Fabric attached to a long Boom

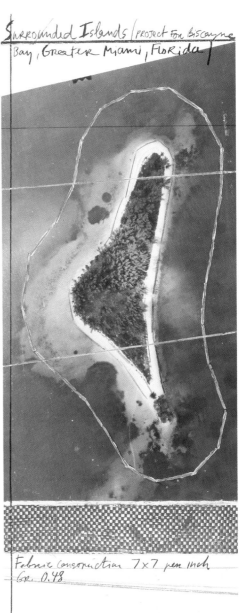

Handwritten annotations on image:
Surrounded Islands / Project For Biscayne Bay, Greater Miami, Florida
Fabric Construction 7 x 7 per inch
Gr. 0.48
Christo 1983

The Christos' "soft intrusion into the life of the metropolis" (as Werner Spies aptly put it) was completed on May 7, 1983, and the eleven islands in the area of Bakers Haulover Cut, Broad Causeway, 79th Street Causeway, Julia Tuttle Causeway and Venetian Causeway were surrounded with 60 hectares of pink woven polypropylene fabric covering the surface of the water, floating and extending 60 meters out from each island into Biscayne Bay. The fabric had been sewn into 79 patterns to follow the contours of the islands, and this work, done at the rented Hialeah factory, took from November 1982 till April 1983. A flotation strip was sewn into each seam, and, at the Opa Locka Blimp hangar, the sewn sections were accordion-folded to ease the subsequent unfurling on the water. This unfurling was begun on May 4, and, once the work was accomplished, the *Surrounded Islands* were tended day and night by over a hundred monitors in inflatable dinghies.

The impact of this remarkable project went far beyond the local scene – though no doubt the many who beheld the sight for themselves during the two weeks of installation were left with an impression permanently engraved upon their minds. On the spot the Christos' project created a two-

Surrounded Islands, Project for Biscayne Bay, Greater Miami, Florida
Collage, 1983, in two parts
Pencil, fabric, pastel, charcoal, crayon, enamel paint, aerial photograph and fabric sample,
71 x 56 and 71 x 28 cm
New York, Collection Jeanne-Claude Christo

PAGE 58:

Surrounded Islands, Project for Biscayne Bay, Greater Miami, Florida
Drawing, 1983, in two parts
Pencil, charcoal, pastel, crayon, enamel paint, aerial photograph and fabric sample,
244 x 38 and 244 x 106.6 cm
New York, Collection Simon Chaput

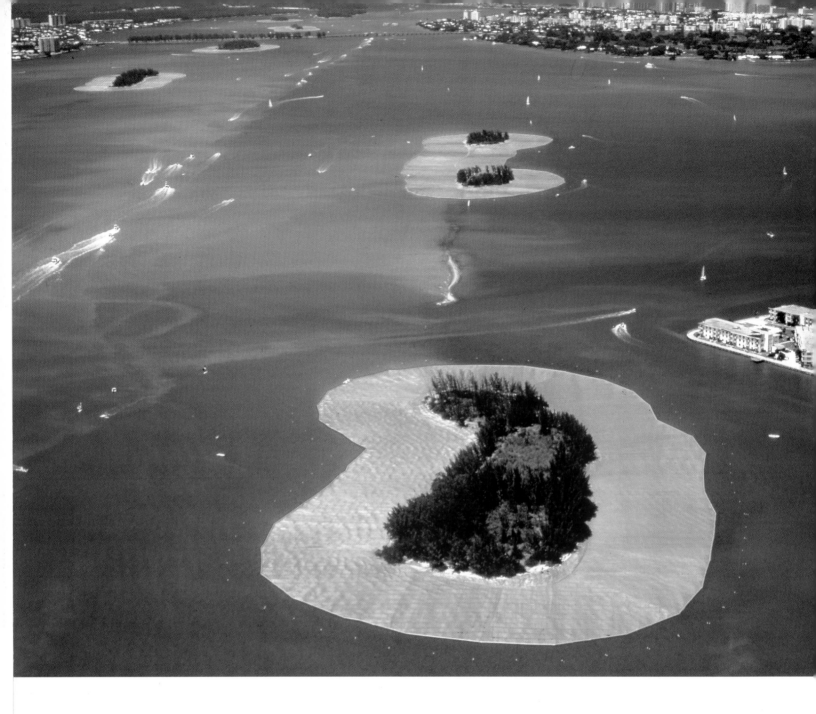

Surrounded Islands, Biscayne Bay, Greater Miami, Florida, 1980–1983
603,850 square meters of fabric

PAGE 63:

Surrounded Islands, Biscayne Bay, Greater Miami, Florida, 1983 (aerial view)
603,850 square meters of fabric

them as charlatans, the use of powerful allies makes the best of sense. Exposure and controversy are, quite simply, a means of generating the interest, and thus the funds, that go into the increasingly costly and complex projects conceived by the Christos, man and wife. (And the money the Christos put into their projects frequently finds its way into the coffers of local communities, thus providing them with the multiple benefits of art, publicity, and plain cash.)

The Christos were still finding that objections usually accused them of frivolity, their projects of not being art, accusations that came mostly from other artists. And the same battles needed to be fought once again over the next project, the *Pont Neuf Wrapped*. Opposition to wrapping the bridge (the oldest in Paris) was strong. Begun under King Henri III, the Pont-Neuf was completed in 1606, during the reign of Henri IV. From 1578 to 1890 the Pont-Neuf underwent continual changes and additions, sometimes of an extravagant sort, such as the construction of shops on the bridge under Jacques Germain Soufflot, or the building, demolition and rebuilding of the substantial rococo structure that housed the Samaritaine's water pump – which was subsequently demolished once again. With so long a tradition, in so tradition-

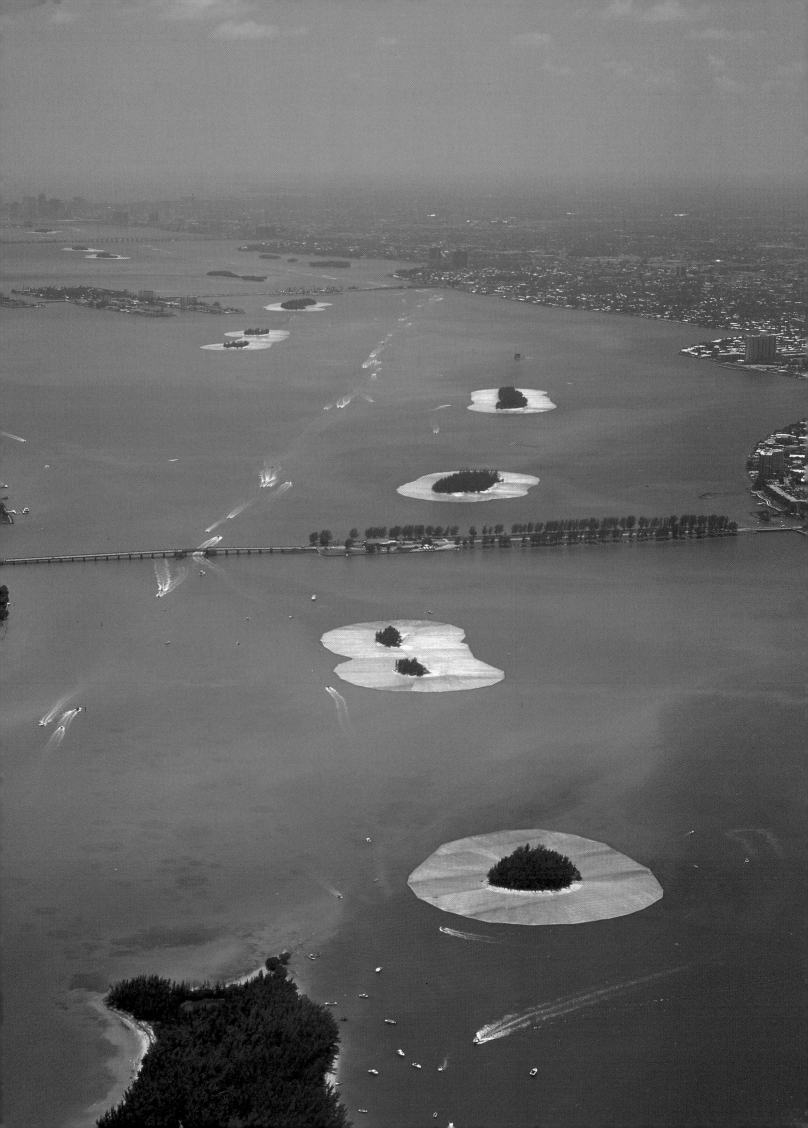

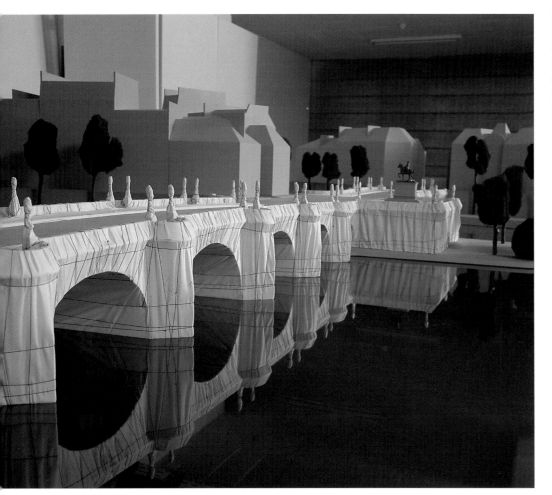

PAGE 65:
The Pont Neuf Wrapped, Project for Paris
Collage, 1985, in two parts
Pencil, fabric, twine, pastel, charcoal, crayon,
aerial photograph and technical data,
30.5 x 77.5 cm and 66.7 x 77.5 cm
New York, Collection Jeanne-Claude Christo

The Pont Neuf Wrapped, Project for Paris
Scale model (detail), 1985
Wood, plexiglass, fabric and twine,
82 x 611 x 478 cm
New York, Collection Jeanne-Claude Christo

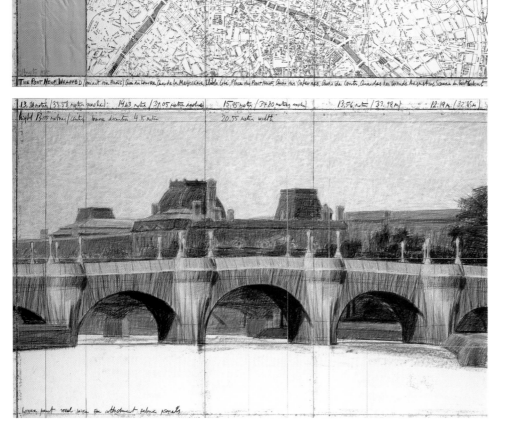

The Pont Neuf Wrapped, Project for Paris
Drawing, 1985, in two parts
Pencil, charcoal, pastel, crayon, map and
fabric sample, 38 x 165 and 106.6 x 165 cm
New York, Collection Jeanne-Claude Christo

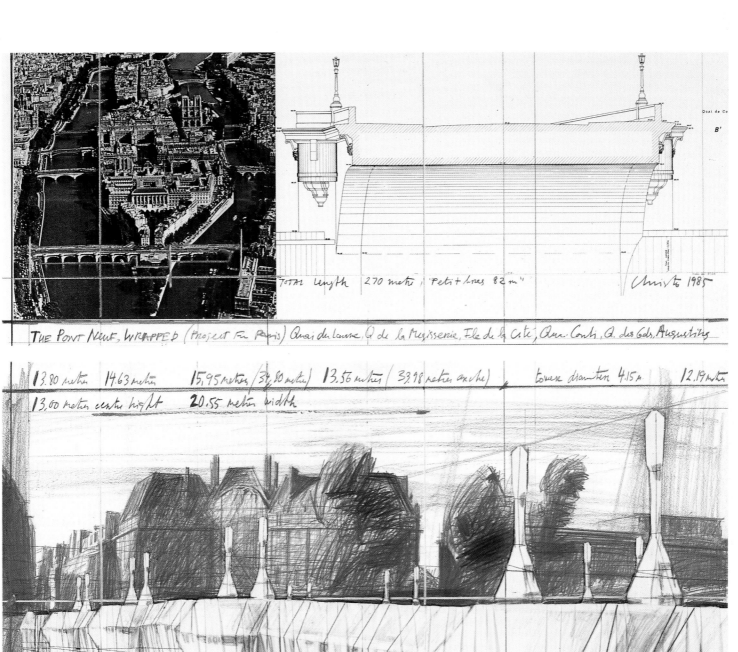

TOTAL length | 270 metre ; "Petit bras 82 m"   Christo 1985

THE PONT NEUF, WRAPPED (Project For Paris) Quai du Louvre, Q. de la Megisserie, Ile de la Cité, Quai Conti, Q. des Gds. Augustins

13.80 metre   14.63 metre   15.95 metre (34.80 metre)   13.56 metres (33.98 metres arche)   tower diameter 4.15 m.   12.19 metres
13.00 metre centre hight   20.55 metre width

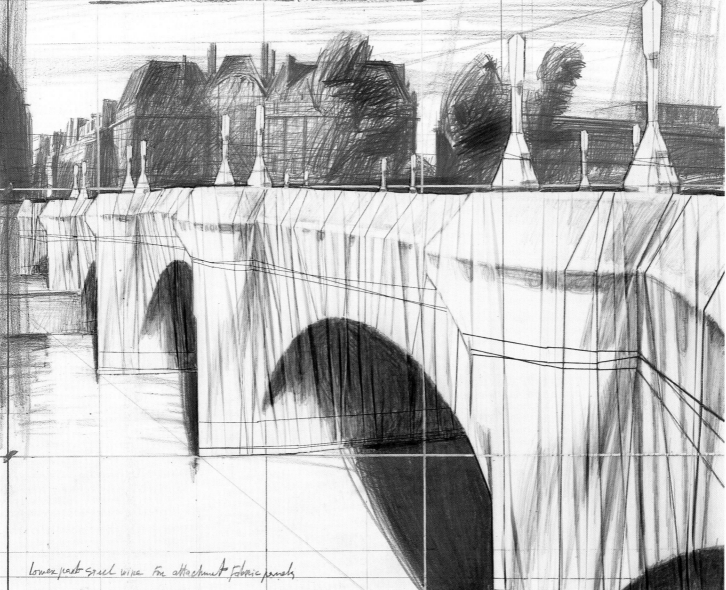

lower part steel wire for attachment fabric panels

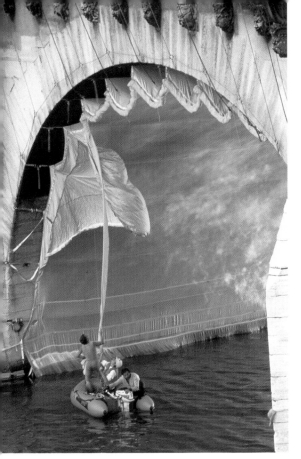

The Pont Neuf Wrapped, Paris, during installation, September 1985

conscious and great a metropolis as Paris, the Pont-Neuf was naturally at the center of a storm of controversy when the Christos proposed to wrap it.

No other bridge in Paris is so thrilling, so laden with cultural and historical importance. Many artists in the past have painted the bridge, among them J. M. W. Turner, Auguste Renoir, Camille Pissarro, Paul Signac, Pablo Picasso and Albert Marquet, and others. Furthermore, since ancient times, the building of a bridge has had an aura of the religious, and has partaken of ritual significance. Speculation was rife among the controversialists: wrapping the bridge would harm it, or those who crossed it or passed below, or would rob the stone of its original appearance, or would otherwise desecrate a cultural totem. For the Christos, winning approval was an uphill battle that took ten years. They began, as so often, democratically – with the people who lived in the immediate neighborhood, talking to them, persuading them. And their campaign continued all the way to the French President and the Mayor of Paris, both of whom had to give their approval before the project could finally proceed.

At long last, permission was given by Mayor Jacques Chirac, the former premier with presidential ambitions, and by his arch rival, President François Mitterand. After blocking the Rue Visconti with oil barrels, the Christos had repeatedly tried to embark on Parisian projects, but to no avail. Wrapping the Pont-Neuf – which proved a triumphant success in the event – was a gesture, the symbolic repayment of a debt that Christo felt he owed to France, his first true home after his escape from behind the Iron Curtain. The bridge arguably symbolized (among other things) his own crossing from the Communist to the Free World, and his new-found freedom to express himself in art.

On September 22, 1985, a group of 300 professional workers completed the temporary work of art *The Pont Neuf Wrapped* (1975–1985, p.67). They had used nearly 41,000 square meters of woven polyamide fabric, silky in appearance and the color of golden sandstone, and with it they had covered the sides and vaults of the Pont-Neuf's twelve arches (without obstructing river traffic); the parapets to ground level; the sidewalks and curbs (pedestrians walked on the fabric); all the street lamps on both sides of the bridge; the vertical part of the embankment on the western tip of the Ile de la Cité; and the esplanade of the Vert-Galant. The fabric was restrained by 13,076 meters of rope and secured with over twelve tons of steel chains encircling the base of each tower.

The Charpentiers de Paris, headed by Gérard Moulin, with a team of French sub-contractors, were assisted by the team of engineers (Vahé Aprahamian, August L. Huber, James Fuller, John Thompson and Dimiter Zagoroff) who have worked on a number of the Christos' projects, under the direction of Theodore Dougherty. Project director Johannes Schaub had submitted detailed plans and a work method description, which had been approved by the Parisian and state authorities.

And the result? All the detail of the bridge had become invisible – "as if" (wrote Werner Spies) "it had been designed by Adolf Loos, who declared that all ornamentation is a crime". The visual impression made by the wrapped bridge was one of post-modern, aerodynamic architecture that preserved one or two anachronistically medieval features. Those who asked after the point of the enterprise were well answered by one of the Chamonix mountaineers who had been engaged in binding up the vertical walls, and who observed that he really had no idea why he scaled the summits of mountains, either. The thing must be its own vindication: it is done because it is possible to do it. That bridges have always stood for the transitory and passing in life, and for the perilous crossing of the abyss, is a symbolic meaning that will appeal to some, perhaps in the same way as the statistics appeal to

PAGE 67:
The Pont Neuf Wrapped, Paris, 1975–1985
Polyamide fabric and rope

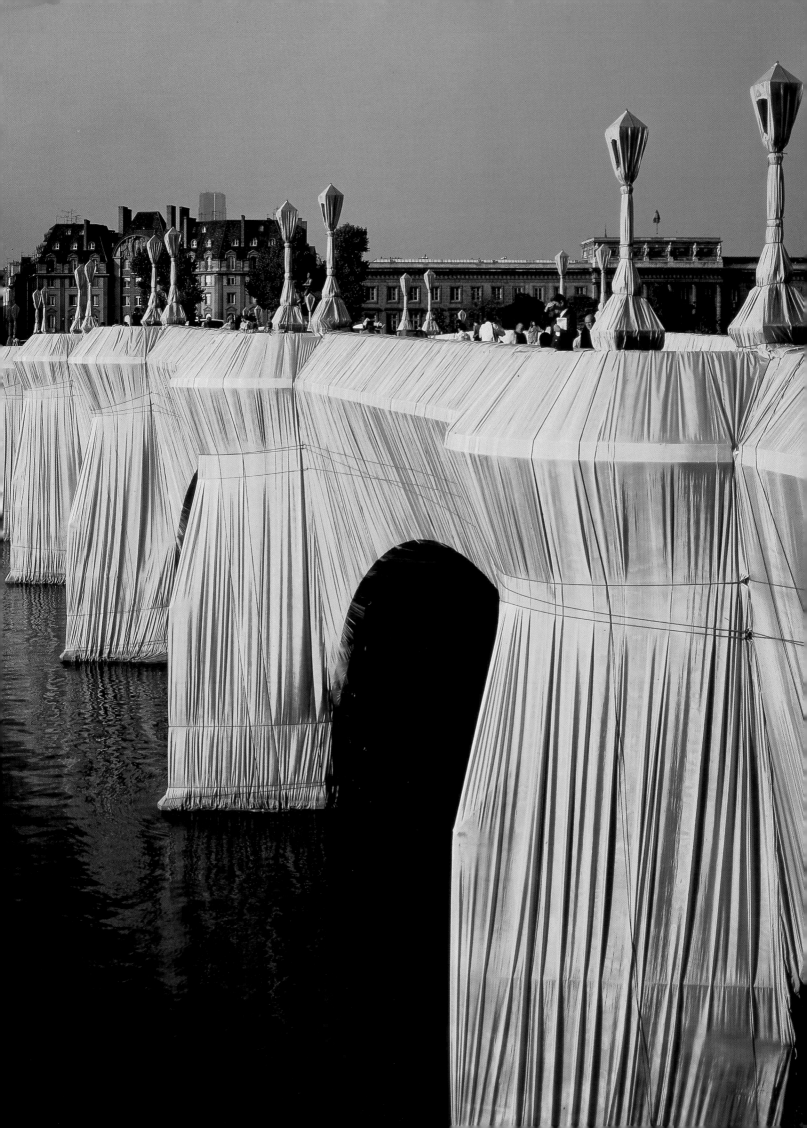

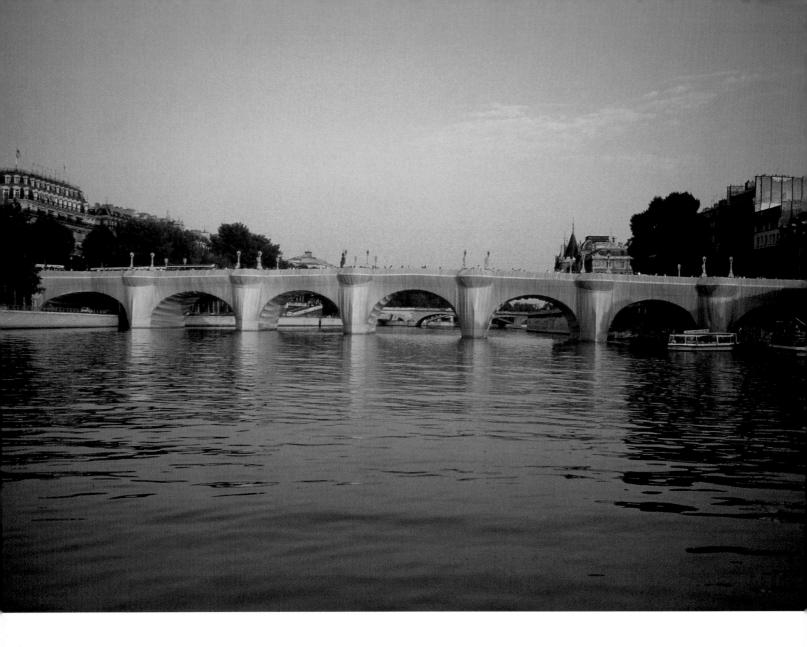

The Pont Neuf Wrapped, Paris, 1975–1985
Polyamide fabric and rope

PAGE 69:
The Pont Neuf Wrapped, Paris, 1975–1985
aerial view

others; but the Christos' work, making its most complete and memorable impact on site, to those who travel to see it, tends to insist on its own simplicity, despite the complexity of the operations involved. After the completion of wrapping the bridge, even those who first opposed it were astonished and impressed by the great artistic beauty of the project.

Discussing his work with Masahiko Yanagi for an exhibition catalog of his work (Annely Juda Gallery, London, 1988), Christo said: "I see my projects as having two major periods or steps. One I like to think of as the 'software period' and the other as the 'hardware period'. The software period is when the project is in my drawings, propositions, scale models, legal applications, and technical data. That software period is the more invisible because there are only projections of how the bridge will look. This is different from an architect or a bridge builder, for example, who can refer to previous skyscrapers or previous bridges, and they can make their work look about the same. But because we had never wrapped a bridge, each proposition is unique, even for us [...] Really how the bridge would look at the end was not defined in 1975 when I had the idea [...] The realized work of art, *The Pont Neuf Wrapped*, is the accumulation of the anticipation and the expectation of a variety of forces: formal, visual, symbolic, political, social, and historical. This is why when we arrive at the hardware period – the second part – the physical making of the work is probably the most enjoyable and rewarding because it is the crowning of many years of expectation. The hardware period is very much like a mirror, showing

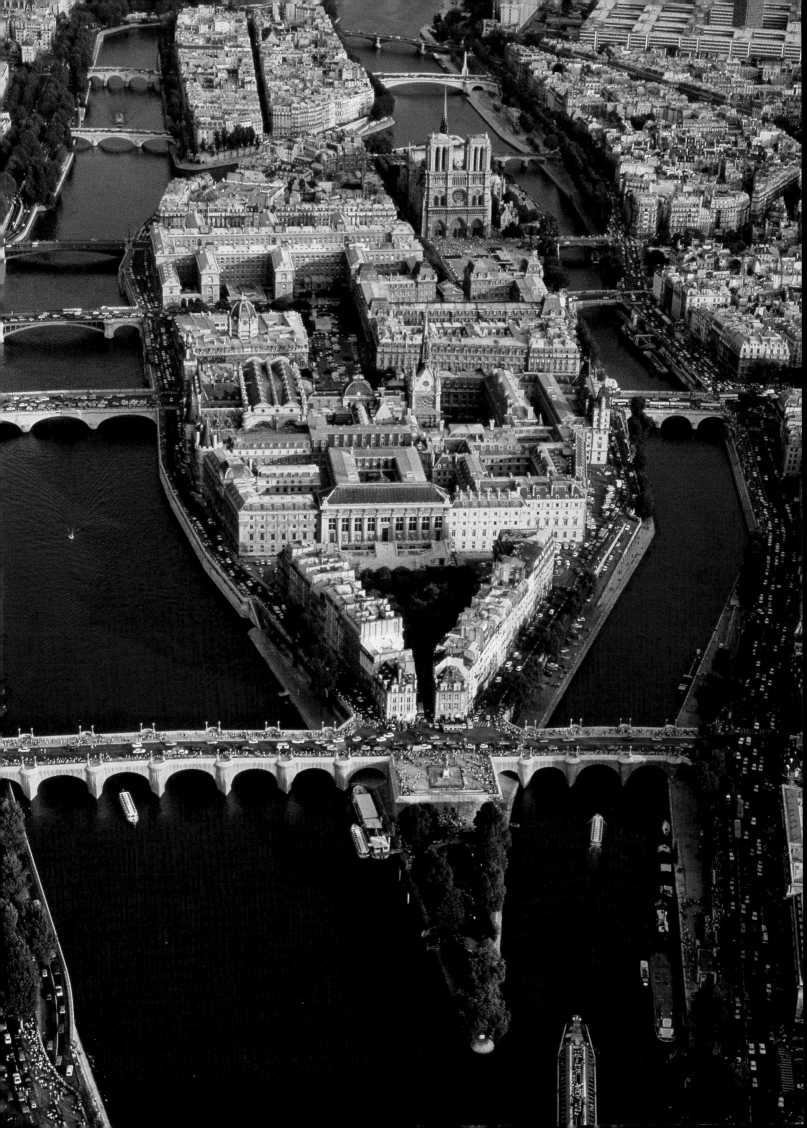

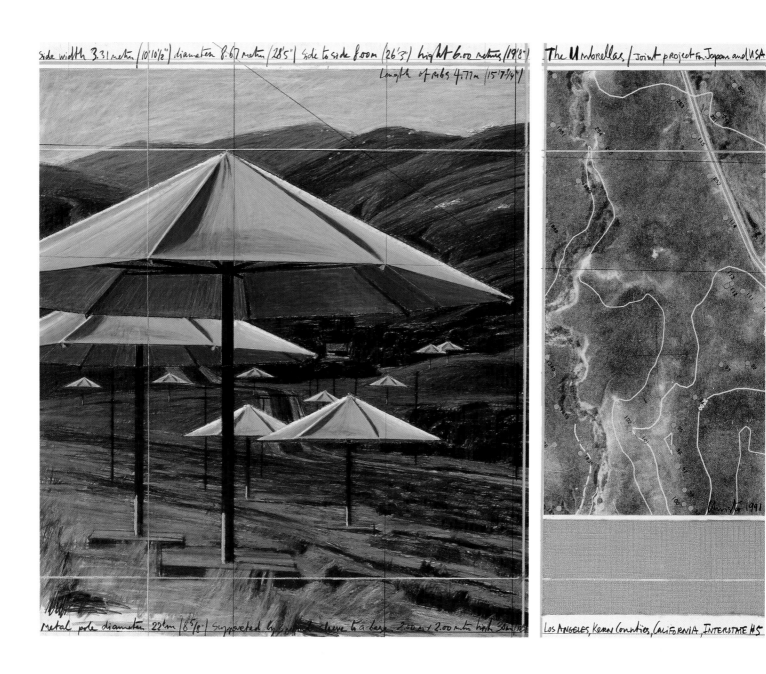

side width 3.31 meter /10'10½"/ diameter 8.67 meter /28'5"/ Side to side 8.00m /26'3"/ height 6.00 meters /19'8"/
Length of ribs 4.77m /15'7¾"/

The Umbrellas / Joint project for Japan and USA

metal pole diameter 22cm /8⅝"/ supported by special sleeve to a base 2.00m x 2.00 meter high 30cm/1'/

Los Angeles, Kern Counties, California, Interstate #5

The Umbrellas, Joint Project for Japan and USA
Collage, 1991, in two parts
Pencil, fabric, pastel, charcoal, crayon, enamel paint,
topographic map and fabric sample,
77.5 x 66.7 cm and 77.5 x 30.5 cm
New York, Collection Jeanne-Claude Christo

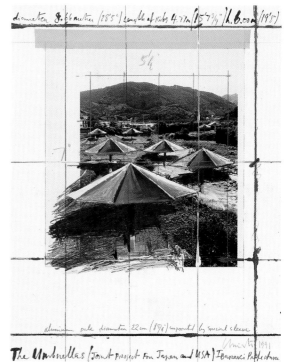

diameter 8.66 meter /28'5"/ Length of ribs 4.77m /15'7¾"/ h. 6.00 m /19'8"/

The Umbrellas /Joint project for Japan and USA/ Ibaraki Prefecture

aluminum pole diameter 22cm /8⅝"/ supported by special sleeve

The Umbrellas, Joint Project for Japan and USA
Collage, 1991
Pencil, enamel paint, photograph by Wolfgang Volz,
charcoal, crayon and tape, 35.5 x 28 cm
New York, Collection Jeanne-Claude Christo

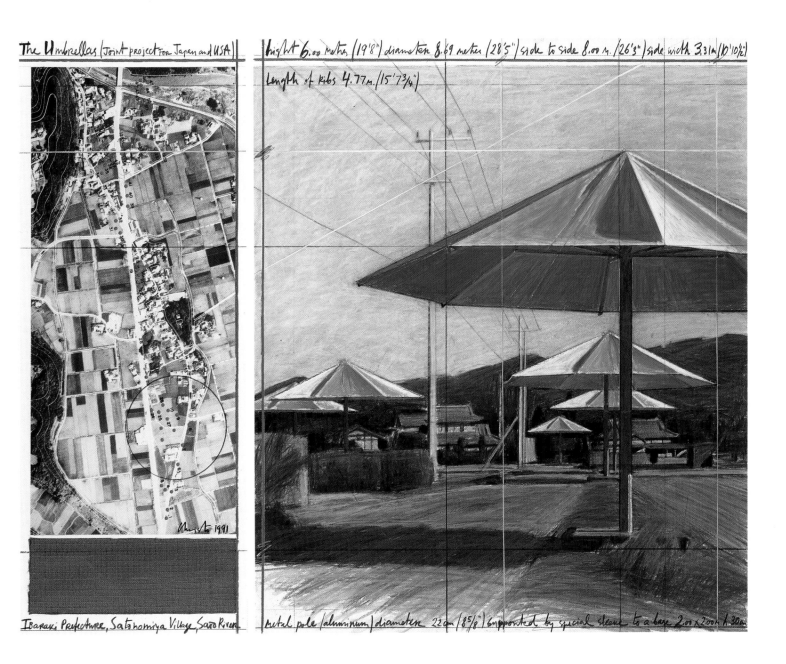

The Umbrellas (Joint project for Japan and USA)

hight 6.00 meter (19'8") diameter 8.69 meter (28'5") side to side 8.00 m (26'3") side width 3.31m (10'10½")

Length of ribs 4.77m (15'7¾")

Ibaraki Prefecture, Satomomiya Village, Sato River

metal pole (aluminium) diameter 22 cm (8⅝") supported by special sleave to a base 2.00 x 2.00 h 30 cm

The Umbrellas, Joint Project for Japan and USA
Collage, 1991, in two parts
Pencil, fabric, pastel, charcoal, crayon, aerial photograph
and fabric sample,
77.5 x 30.5 and 77.5 x 66.7 cm
New York, Collection Jeanne-Claude Christo

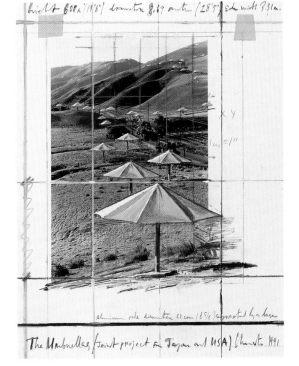

The Umbrellas, Joint Project for Japan and USA
Collage, 1991
Pencil, crayon, enamel paint, charcoal, photograph by
Wolfgang Volz, ballpoint pen and tape, 35.5 x 28 cm
New York, Collection Jeanne-Claude Christo

71

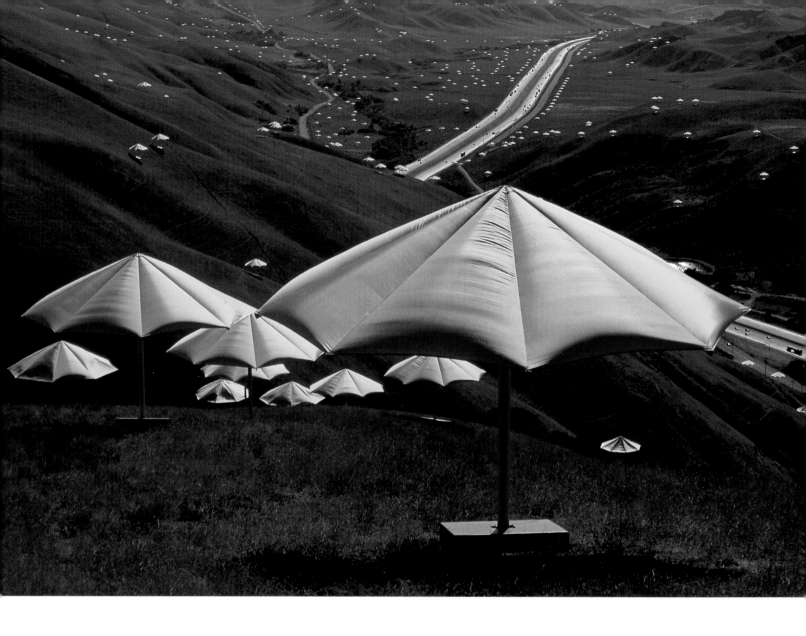

The Umbrellas, Japan – USA,
1984–1991 (California Site)
1,760 yellow umbrellas – each 6 m high and
8.66 m in diameter

what we have worked at. The final object is really the ending of that dynamic idea about the work." In this account, Christo spells out an underlying appeal present throughout their work, an appeal to our love of contingency and flux and of gradual evolution.

The most ambitious and costly project in the Christos' life as artists to date has been *The Umbrellas, Japan–USA* (1984–1991, p. 70–77). For the first time, a project was brought to fruition in two locations simultaneously, making one work of art. The cost of the project was $26 million, and the logistics were nothing short of staggering. In Japan there were 1,340 blue umbrellas; in the USA, 1,760 yellow umbrellas. Each umbrella was 6 meters high including the base and 8.66 meters in diameter, and weighed about 200 kilograms. A total volume of 7,600 liters of paint was used; the structural aluminum materials included a total length of almost 18 kilometers of umbrella poles, almost 25,000 umbrella ribs and about as many struts, and 410,000 square meters of fabric in all. Needless to say, the usual permissions had to be sought – from seventeen government and local community authorities in Japan, and twenty-seven in the United States, not to mention over 450 individual rice farmers and other landowners.

When all was done, when all the hard preparation had been invested and the costs borne, the umbrellas were ready to be unfurled – in rice fields, in a river, on hillsides, and in villages. "At sunrise on October 9, 1991, 1,880 workers began to open the 3,100 umbrellas in Ibaraki and California, in the

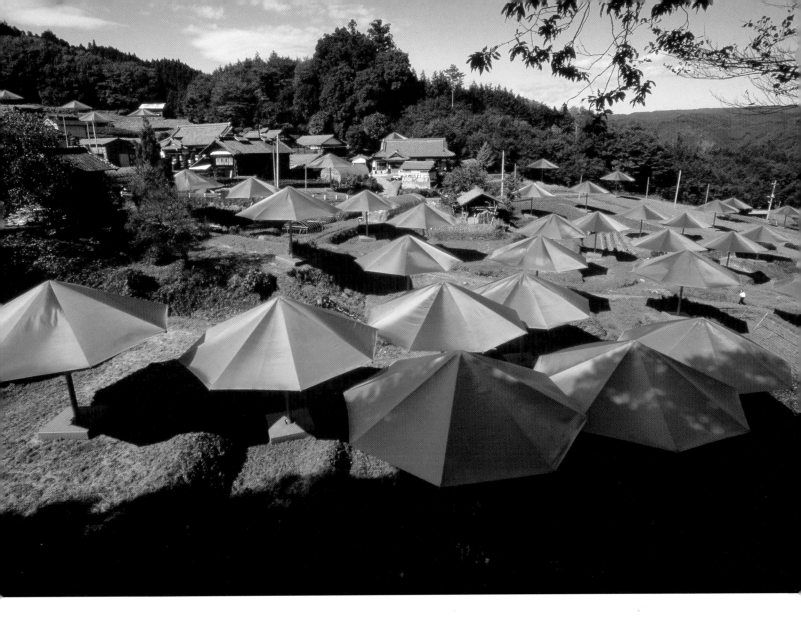

presence of the artists," ran the Christos' bulletin. "This Japan-USA temporary work of art reflected the similarities and differences in the ways of life and the use of the land in two inland valleys, one 19 kilometers long (12 miles) in Japan, and the other 29 kilometers long (18 miles) in the USA."

The fabric, aluminum superstructure and steel frame bases, as well as the anchors, base supports and other components, had been made by 11 manufacturers in Japan, the USA, Germany and Canada. All of the umbrellas were assembled at Bakersfield in California, and from there the 1,340 blue umbrellas were shipped to Japan.

Beginning in December 1990, with a work-force totalling 500, Muto Construction Co. Ltd. in Ibaraki, and A. L. Huber & Son in California, installed the earth anchors and bases, with work continuing through to September 1991. At that point, from September 19 to October 7, an additional construction "force" (the word is Christo's – the husband of the French general's daughter seems often to approach his tasks in an almost military style) transported the umbrellas to their bases, bolted them in, and raised them to an upright but closed position. This team was joined on October 4 by over 900 further workers in each country – students, farm workers and friends – to complete installation. (Removal began on October 27; the land was restored to its original condition, and all the materials recycled.)

"The umbrellas," wrote the Christos, "free-standing dynamic modules, reflected the availability of the land in each valley, creating an invitational

The Umbrellas, Japan – USA, 1984–1991
(Ibaraki, Japan Site)
1,340 blue umbrellas – each 6 m high and 8.66 m in diameter

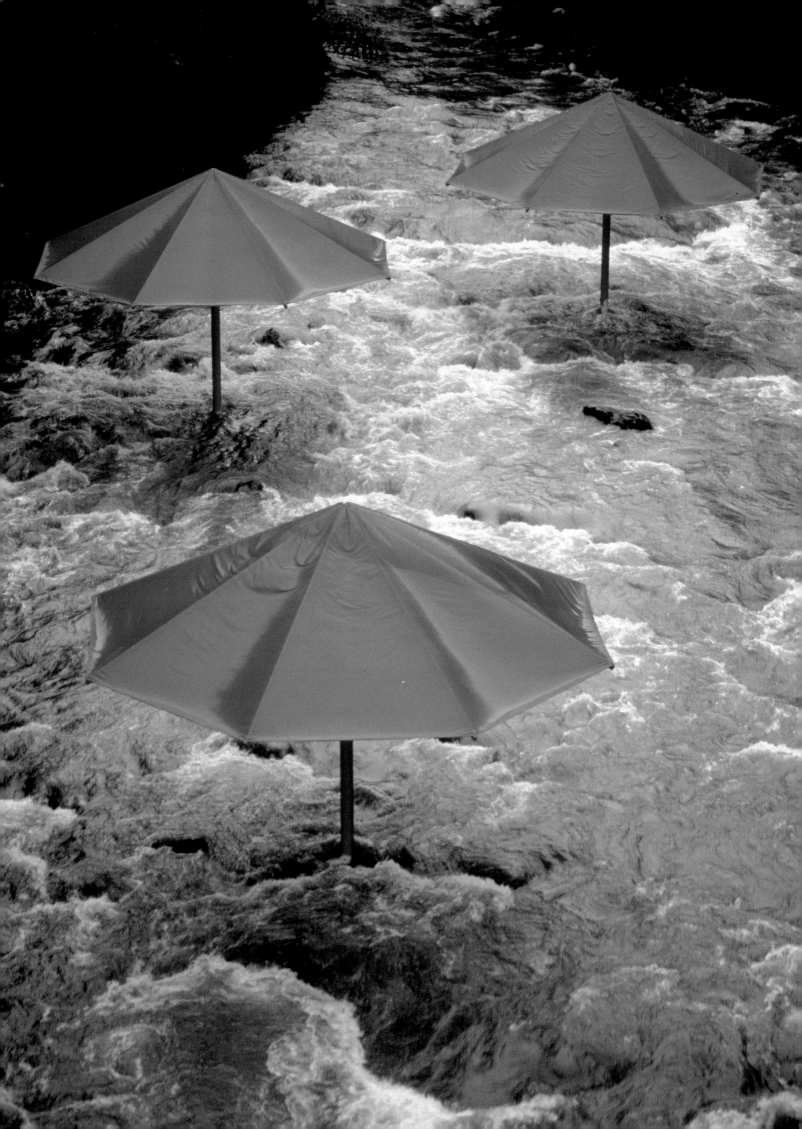

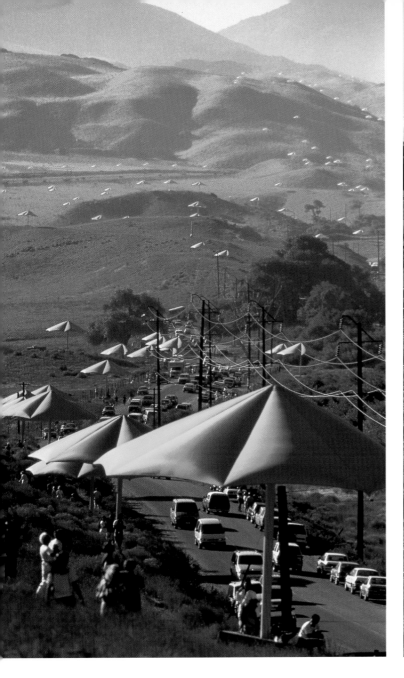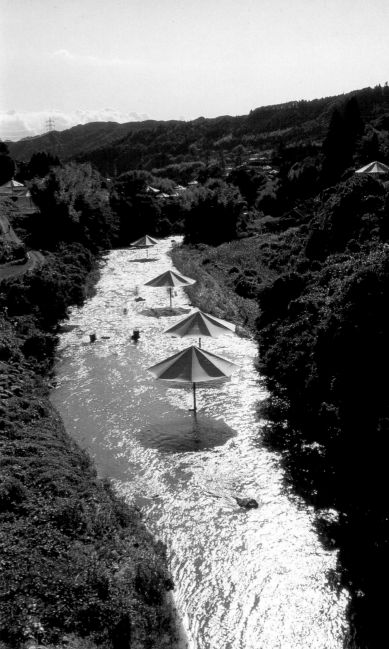

inner space, as houses without walls, or temporary settlements [...] In the precious and limited space of Japan, the umbrellas were positioned intimately, close together and sometimes following the geometry of the rice fields. In the luxuriant vegetation enriched by water year round, the umbrellas were blue. In the California vastness of uncultivated grazing land, the configuration of the umbrellas was whimsical and spreading in every direction. The brown hills in California were covered by blond grass, and, in that dry landscape, the umbrellas were yellow."

It has often been suggested – with the history of the Medicis in mind, or William Golding's novel *The Spire* – that the creation of great art is inseparable from death or sacrifice. It would be tactless to suggest that the two tragic accidents that took a life at each site fitted into this pattern; the Christos shared the widespread distress. But the joy was widespread too: *The Umbrellas, Japan–USA* were a presence of simple grace and startling beauty – and, incidentally, a reminder that there was far more to the Christos' art than the wrapping they had become so closely associated with. The *Valley Curtain* (1970–1972, p.47), *Running Fence* (1972–1976, p.51), *Surrounded Islands* (1980–1983, p.63) and *The Umbrellas, Japan–USA* were a new departure that took them into resplendent realms far beyond wrapping.

LEFT:
The Umbrellas, Japan – USA, 1984–1991
(California Site)

RIGHT:
The Umbrellas, Japan – USA, 1984–1991
(Ibaraki, Japan Site)

PAGE 74:
The Umbrellas, Japan – USA, 1984–1991
(Ibaraki, Japan Site),
90 blue umbrellas were in the Sato River.

PAGE 76:
The Umbrellas, Japan – USA, 1984–1991
(Ibaraki, Japan Site)

PAGE 77:
The Umbrellas, Japan – USA, 1984–1991
(California Site)

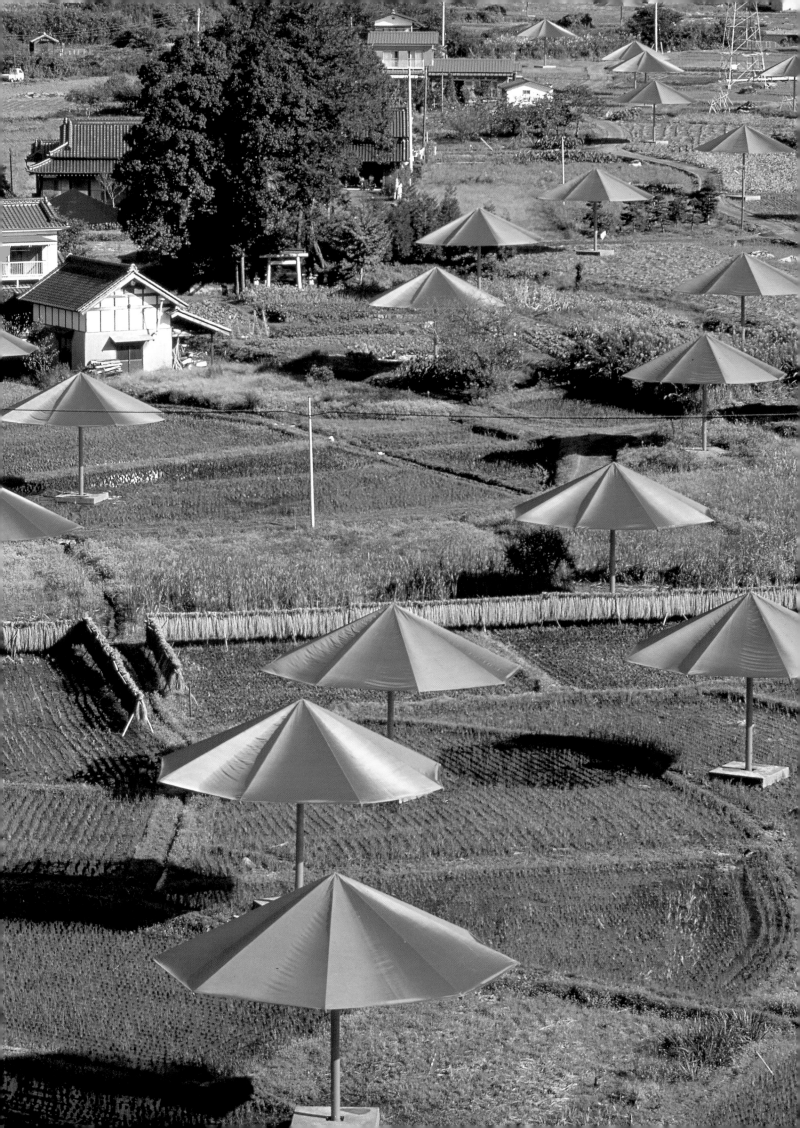

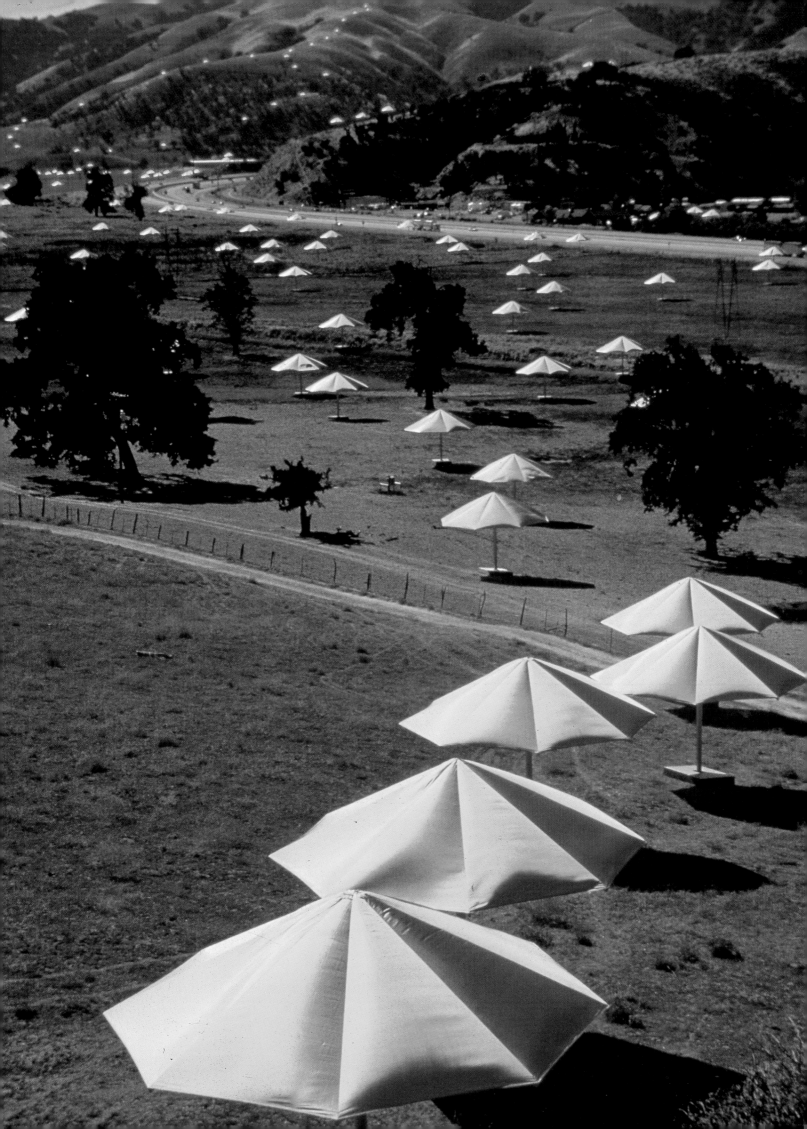

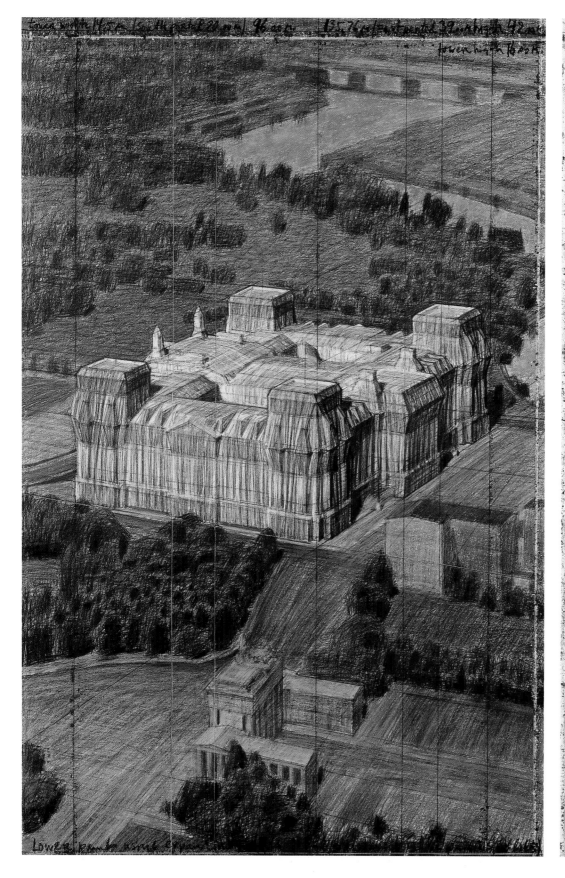

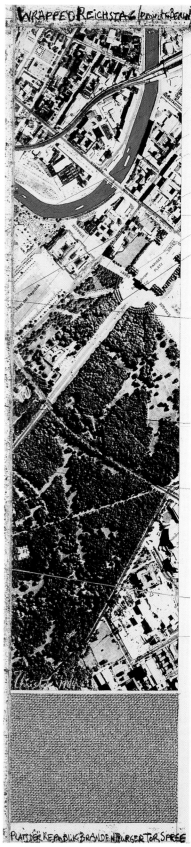

"A postcard from Berlin"
The Reichstag

The long saga of the Reichstag project began in September 1971. While working on the *Valley Curtain* project (1970–1972, p. 47) in Colorado, the Christos received a postcard of the Reichstag from Michael S. Cullen, an American living in Berlin, suggesting that they wrap either the Reichstag or the Brandenburg Gate. In November that year, Jeanne-Claude wrote to Cullen informing him that the artists were indeed interested in the idea, but were currently concentrating on the *Valley Curtain* project.

On December 4, 1971, Christo and Cullen met for the first time, in Zurich. Christo, invariably a scrupulous planner, decided that permission should be obtained before tackling the technical problems that needed solving. At that time, it was hoped that the project might go ahead in the spring and summer of 1973.

Christo's first drawing of a *Wrapped Reichstag, Project for Berlin* dates back to the spring of 1972, at a time when he was completing the *Valley Curtain* in Colorado and planning the *Running Fence*. An office for the Reichstag project was established in Berlin by Michael Cullen.

In those busy years, the Christos realised two further projects – *The Wall – Wrapped Roman Wall* (p. 49) in Rome in 1974, and the *Ocean Front* (p. 48) in Newport, Rhode Island, also in 1974 – and began planning the Pont-Neuf wrapping. It was not till February 12, 1976, that they visited Berlin for the first time, together with Wolfgang Volz, the photographer who has been the constant companion documenting their projects throughout their evolution and on completion. With Michael Cullen they examined the Reichstag building, and Christo gave his first press conference, explaining among other things that the project (as always) would be entirely financed by the Christos, from the sale of drawings and collages.

The artist began meeting members of the Berlin CDU (Christian Democratic Union) and SPD (Social Democratic Party), and a meeting was arranged with the SPD President of the Bundestag, Annemarie Renger, in June 1976. Renger pointed out that a decision could not be taken by herself alone; the Allies (Soviet, American, British and French) would have a say – and, in any case, with West German elections looming in November 1976, the parties had other things on their minds.

The Christos continued with the *Running Fence* in California, and then with the *Wrapped Walk Ways* (p. 55) in Kansas City, Missouri. Meanwhile, in Germany, Karl Carstens of the CDU became the new President of the Bundestag. After meeting the Christos, West Berlin's Mayor Klaus Schütz decided to give their project his support; but a vote in the Presidium of the Bundestag in January 1977 went against it.

Persistence has always been one of the Christos' most striking characteristics. Far from giving up, they next met former West German Chancellor

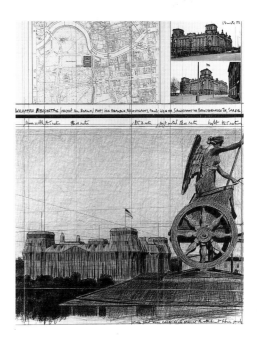

Wrapped Reichstag, Project for Berlin
Collage, 1992, in two parts
Pencil, fabric, twine, pastel, charcoal, crayon, map and technical data, in two parts:
30.5 x 77.5 cm and 66.7 x 77.5 cm
Berlin, Private collection

PAGE 78:
Wrapped Reichstag, Project for Berlin
Drawing, 1994, in two parts
Pencil, charcoal, pastel and crayon
165 x 106.6 cm and 165 x 38 cm
Tarrytown, N.Y., Stinnes Corporation

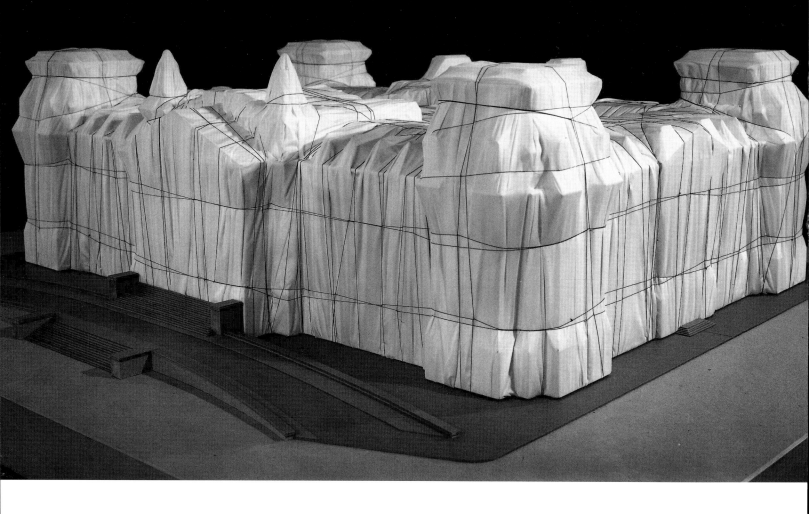

Wrapped Reichstag, Project for Berlin
Scale model, 1978
Fabric, twine, wood, cardboard, masonite and
paint, 46 x 244 x 152 cm
The Lilja Art Fund Foundation

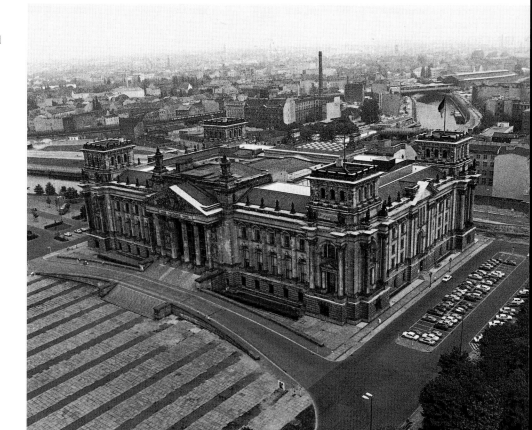

Aerial view of the Reichstag, west façade
East Berlin in the background, 1986
New York, Collection Jeanne-Claude Christo

80

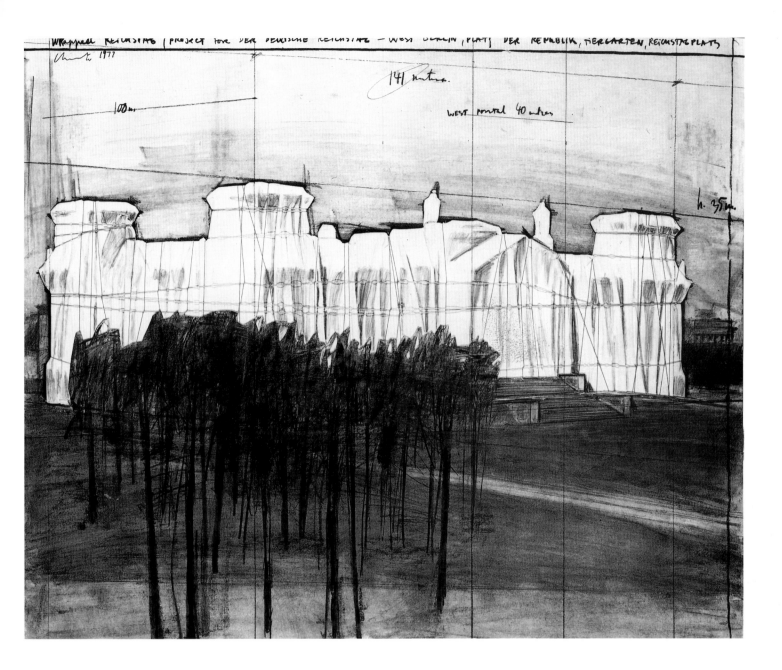

Willy Brandt, one of the country's most distinguished statesmen, Chairman of the SPD and a former Mayor of West Berlin. Brandt too promised his support for the project. At Willy Brandt's suggestion, a collage of the Reichstag project was lent to him to hang in his office for callers to see. A meeting followed with the Allies, who found that the issue of wrapping the Reichstag was a purely internal, German question that did not concern them. As long as there were two partitioned Germanies, however, such questions were potential landmines; and President of the German Bundestag Karl Carstens, whilst reiterating his respect for the artists themselves, pronounced a formal refusal on the project, fearing complications with East-Germany.

The new Mayor of West Berlin, Dietrich Stobbe, was the next prominent figure to come out in favor of the Reichstag wrapping, describing the project as a "positive provocation".

In November 1977 the Christos held their first exhibition of collages and drawings relating to the *Wrapped Reichstag, Project for Berlin* at the Annely Juda Gallery in London. Other projects were occupying them too, though; they typically work on a number of ideas concurrently, and at that point in the late 1970s, alongside completion of the *Wrapped Walk Ways* (p. 55), they began planning *The Mastaba Project for Abu Dhabi* (1978, p.

Wrapped Reichstag, Project for Berlin
Collage, 1977
Fabric, twine, pencil, pastel and charcoal,
22 x 28 cm
Hamburg, Collection G. Bucerius

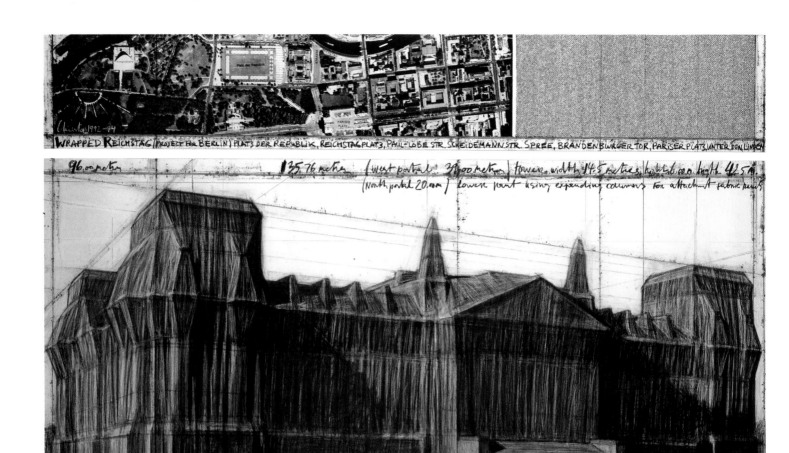

Wrapped Reichstag, Project for Berlin
Drawing, 1992–1994, in two parts
Pencil, charcoal, pastel, crayon, aerial photograph and fabric sample,
38 x 244 and 106.6 x 244 cm
New York, Collection Jeanne-Claude Christo

88) and *The Gates* (p. 90) for Central Park in New York. Completion of the *Surrounded Islands* (1980–1983, p. 56) followed in 1983. As we have seen, they were also exhibiting and lecturing in the early 1980s – importantly, in terms of its revival of public interest in the Reichstag project, they had a show of urban projects at Cologne's Museum Ludwig in September 1981 and subsequently in Berlin. A meeting followed with Richard von Weizsäcker, who was to become President of West Germany in 1984; he too promised his support.

On another front, in 1984 Jacques Chirac gave the go-ahead for the *Pont-Neuf* project (p. 67) in Paris, after nine years of arduous negotiations. The Christos concentrated on that work and on initial preparations for *The Umbrellas*, while elsewhere the fortunes of German politicians brought yeas and nays in quick succession: Bundestag President Rainer Barzel (CDU), who had supported the Reichstag project, resigned and was succeeded by Philipp Jenninger, who withheld his support; in September 1985 West German Chancellor Helmut Kohl came out firmly against the project; and when Rita Süssmuth succeeded Jenninger as Bundestag President in November 1988 she intimated that the Reichstag project appealed to her, though at that point without making a firm commitment.

The great turning point came with the fall of the Berlin Wall on November 9, 1989. The Christos in the United States shared the excitement of the people of Berlin, and felt confident now that the time for the project was nearing. On October 3, 1990, Germany was reunited, and on June 20 the following year the Bundestag voted to make Berlin the capital of the restored nation once more and to move the seat of government there from Bonn. In 1992 the Christos' influential supporter Willy Brandt died. In 1991 Rita

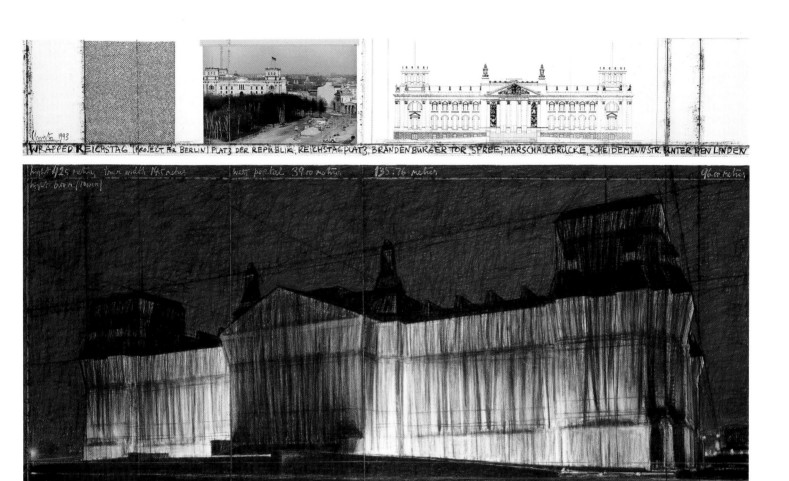

WRAPPED REICHSTAG (PROJECT FOR BERLIN) PLATZ DER REPUBLIK, REICHSTAGPLATZ, BRANDENBURGER TOR, SPREE, MARSCHALLBRÜCKE, SCHEIDEMANN STR. UNTER DEN LINDEN

Süssmuth declared her full support and assured them that she would fight hard to see the project realized. That was two months after *The Umbrellas* project was completed in Japan and the USA; from then on, though the Christos were as engaged with other ideas as ever, their main concern was to press ahead with the Reichstag project. Rita Süssmuth quickly proved a conspicuous ally, and in January 1993 opened a Christo exhibition at the Marstall Art Academy in Berlin – on the evening of the very day that the jury met to decide on architectural proposals for the renovation of the Reichstag.

Days later, on January 11, 1993, Chancellor Kohl and CDU/CSU Bundestag chief whip Wolfgang Schäuble made a public statement of their opposition to the Christos' proposal. Before the month was out, though, the architectural jury came out in favor of the Reichstag wrapping, in a bulletin issued on January 29, and sent a recommendation to that effect to the Bundestag.

Meanwhile, Rita Süssmuth had approved the exhibition of a scale model of the project alongside the architectural designs for renovation and, on March 22, opened the show in the lobby of the Bundestag. It is worth stressing that Rita Süssmuth, as President of the Bundestag, had the power to suppress the project single-handedly (as four of her predecessors in office had done); similarly, she had the power to approve it alone, but refrained from doing so for the excellent political reason that it would be better for the Christos' project to win a majority of the Members of Parliament.

Finally, on February 25, 1994, the Bundestag voted by a large majority to give the Christos permission to proceed. The vote was 292 in favour, 223 against, with 9 abstentions. It had been a long, hard struggle, involving

Wrapped Reichstag, Project for Berlin
Drawing, 1993, in two parts
Pencil, charcoal, pastel, crayon, photograph by Wolfgang Volz, fabric sample, tape and technical data, 38 x 244 cm and 106.6 x 244cm
Berlin, Collection Carl Flach

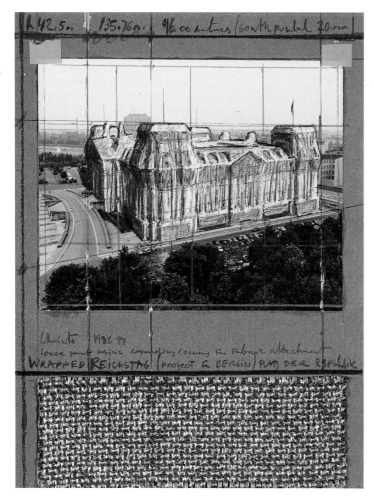

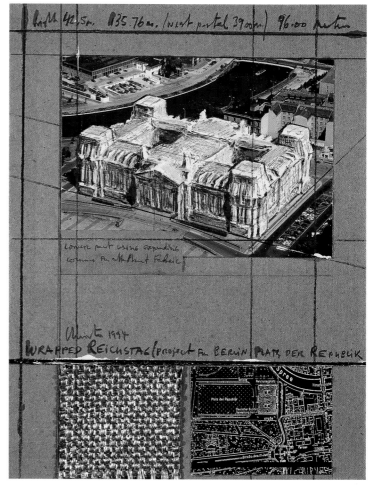

LEFT:
Wrapped Reichstag, Project for Berlin
Collage, 1986–1994
Pencil, enamel paint, crayon, charcoal, photograph by Michael Cullen, ballpoint pen, tape and fabric sample on brown-grey cardboard, 28 x 21.5 cm
Bonn, Collection Volker Adolphs

RIGHT:
Wrapped Reichstag, Project for Berlin
Collage, 1994
Pencil, enamel paint, charcoal, postcard, crayon, ball point pen, map, fabric sample on brown-grey cardboard, 28 x 21.5 cm
Knokke, Collection Guy Pieters

many months of lobbying and patient debate, and taxing the diplomatic skills and charismatic resources of the Christos to the full. For thirty years, Christo told me, they had created art works that were visually exciting. "We are not tragic persons. We do not do tragic things. The Reichstag will be no different. We make very stimulating things. Unlike steel, or stone, or wood, the fabric catches the physicality of the wind, the sun. They are refreshing, and then they are quickly gone."

At the time of writing, it is fair to say that the Christos' Reichstag project enjoys renown even before completion. The argument that it will in some manner strip the building of its dignity is surely wrong-headed; symbolic and historical meanings accrue to a building of the Reichstag's kind, and those meanings will survive a project that is by definition intended to be temporary.

The substance of the Reichstag can only be enhanced by the commitment of dedicated artists to natural beauty and to the fleeting joys that mark the essence of our transient experience of life.

"We would like our project to happen just before the first crane and bull-dozer arrive," observes Christo (referring to the planned architectural changes). "We want to wrap this Reichstag – no other Reichstag – at this unique moment [...] Only we can make the Reichstag a work of art. I say that not one single politician or German will feel ashamed to see a photograph of the *Wrapped Reichstag*. It will be in the books of the history of art."

And what do the artists themselves reply when asked the leading question that has so often been posed – why wrap the Reichstag at all? "I had a special interest in Germany," Christo told me, "because I had my first per-

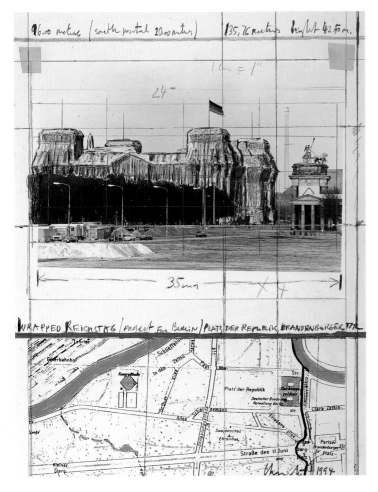

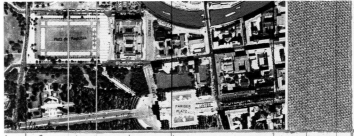

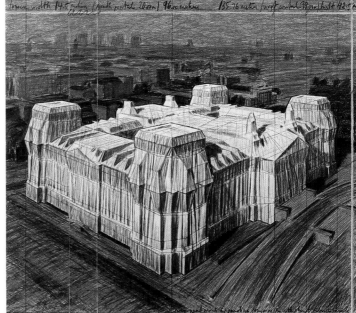

sonal exhibition in Cologne in 1961, and since 1958 I have had a great number of collectors, museum people, critics and friends in Germany who are interested in my work.

"So there was a natural relationship with the German art scene, and German culture in general. Also in 1968 I did a large project in Germany, the *5,600 Cubic Meter Package* at *documenta IV* in Kassel. It is a constant interest of ours, to use a focal point in a city and temporarily transform it in our way. The idea to go to Berlin and to work on the Reichstag project was so much more inspirational because of my links with eastern Europe, and I was in some way expecting that finally I would do a project that could be visible from both East and West Berlin."

Interviewed by Masahiko Yanagi in 1986, Christo furthermore reported: "The first *Running Fence* idea was to have a running fence just along the Berlin Wall, and there are some drawings from between 1970 and 1972 of a fabric fence in West Berlin, hiding the Wall […] that was my first project for Berlin."

"We can now benefit from the Sleeping-Beauty-like quality of the Reichstag," says Christo now. "It was like a tremendous sleeping powerhouse. No German ever believed that, in their lifetime, they would witness the reunification of Germany. The Reichstag was built to be the Parliament of a united Germany. I think all our projects have their own time. Today the site has so much more potential because the entire world questions the future of Europe and where Germany will go from now, in the East-West relations, sitting like a powerhouse of wealth, economic and political weight, and might, that will project tremendous meaning into the twenty-first century."

LEFT:
Wrapped Reichstag, Project for Berlin
Collage, 1994
Pencil, enamel paint, photo by Wolfgang Volz, crayon, charcoal, pastel, map and tape,
35.5 x 28 cm
New York, Collection Jeanne-Claude Christo

RIGHT:
Wrapped Reichstag, Project for Berlin
Collage, 1994, in two parts
Pencil, fabric, twine, pastel, charcoal, crayon, aerial photograph and fabric sample
30.5 x 77.5 and 66.7 x 77.5 cm
New York, Collection Jeanne-Claude Christo

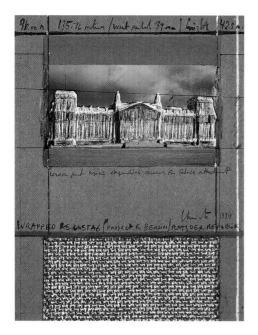

Wrapped Reichstag, Project for Berlin
Collage, 1994
Pencil, enamel paint, postcard, crayon, charcoal, ballpoint pen, brown paper and fabric sample on brown-grey cardboard, 28 x 21.5 cm
Berlin, Private collection

PAGE 87:
Wrapped Reichstag, Project for Berlin
Collage, 1986–1994, in two parts
Pencil, fabric, twine, photograph by Michael Cullen, pastel, charcoal, crayon, tape, map and fabric sample 30.5 x 77.5 and 66.7 x 77.5 cm
New York, Collection Jeanne-Claude Christo

It was the first time ever, that a parliament debated and voted on a work of art, ironically, a work which does not exist. Hostile critics may urge that the Christos' projects express a personal vanity as much as anything else; that temporary wrapping makes no statement whatsoever; and that the Christos' political understanding is of a simple order. But it is rare to find artists whose passionate sense of vocation cannot be mistaken for vanity; wrapping the Reichstag does not claim to be any more than a passing act of grace; and artists whose political understanding has been rich and complex have been few in any age. After all, it is the task of the artist to create art, not to conquer in the debating arenas. In all things, Christo and Jeanne-Claude – alert to the environmental, social, political and other implications of their projects – have remained true to a vision of the artist as a great and above all autonomous maker.

The Reichstag project, not yet achieved at the time of writing, can now become much more than a footnote to the Cold War and be an expression of hope and democratic conviction. For two weeks, the richness of thousands of square meters of silvery fabric, together with the ropes, will create a sumptuous flow of vertical folds highlighting the features and proportions of the structure. The historical importance of fabric needs no stressing: its folds, pleats and draperies have played a significant part in paintings, frescoes, reliefs and sculptures in wood, stone and bronze since the Egyptians and Greeks, and throughout Judaeo-Christian civilization. Veiling carries a charge of sacredness and joyful mystery. The use of fabric for the Reichstag project will be in line with a tradition altogether classical, if unusually so.

High-strength synthetic woven fabric that meets the prescribed standards of fire retardation will be used to wrap the Reichstag, and royal blue dacron rope. Each façade will be covered by eight tailor-made panels. No alterations to the building itself will be made, and every vulnerable statue and ornament will be protected by special, cage-like structures.

The temporary work of art *Wrapped Reichstag* will, as always, be financed entirely by Christo and Jeanne-Claude from the sale of preparatory studies and drawings, scale models and collages, early works and original lithographs.

If all goes as the Christos hope, the wrapped Reichstag will be "a dramatic experience of great beauty". And then all the materials will be removed and recycled – nothing but photographs, films, records, and memories will remain. I shall let Christo himself (interviewed by Michael Farr for *Modern Painters*) have the last word on the vexed issue of the value of so temporary, evanescent a concept of art: "the temporary character of the project is also an esthetic decision to challenge the immortality of art: if art is immortal, if building things in gold, steel and stone is really immortal and will make us live for ever, probably it is more courageous to go away than to stay. All our projects have a very strong self-effacing relationship. The fabric conveys that fragility of the work that will be gone. Our projects have a very strong nomadic quality, like the nomadic tribes that build their tents. By using this vulnerable material, there is a greater urgency to be seen – because tomorrow it will be gone. […] Nobody can buy those works, nobody can own them, nobody can commercialize them, nobody can charge tickets for them. Even ourselves, we do not own these works. The work is about freedom, and freedom is the enemy of possession, and possession is the equal of permanence. This is why the work cannot stay."

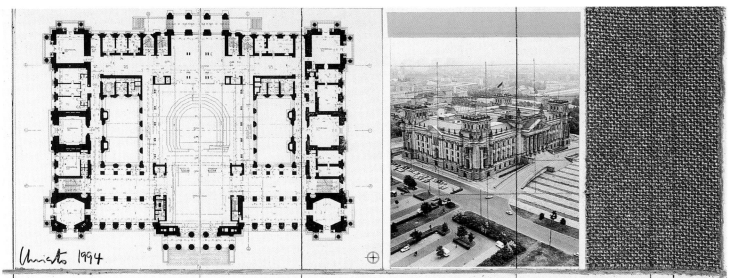

Christo 1994

WRAPPED REICHSTAG (PROJECT FOR BERLIN) PLATZ DER REPUBLIK, SCHEIDEMANNSTR. BRANDENBURGER TOR, UNTER DEN LINDEN

96.00 meters (south portal 20.00 meters) width of tower 14.5 m. 135.76 m. (east portal 39.00 meters
height 42.00 m.

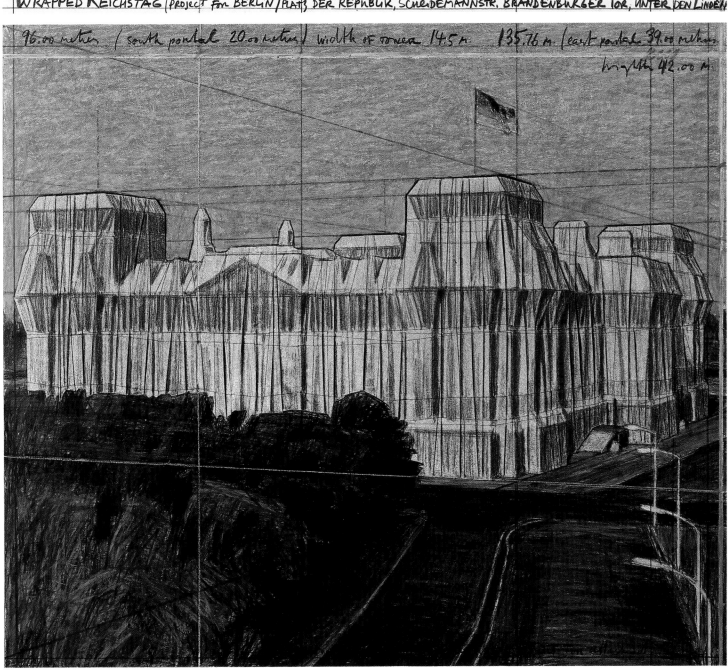

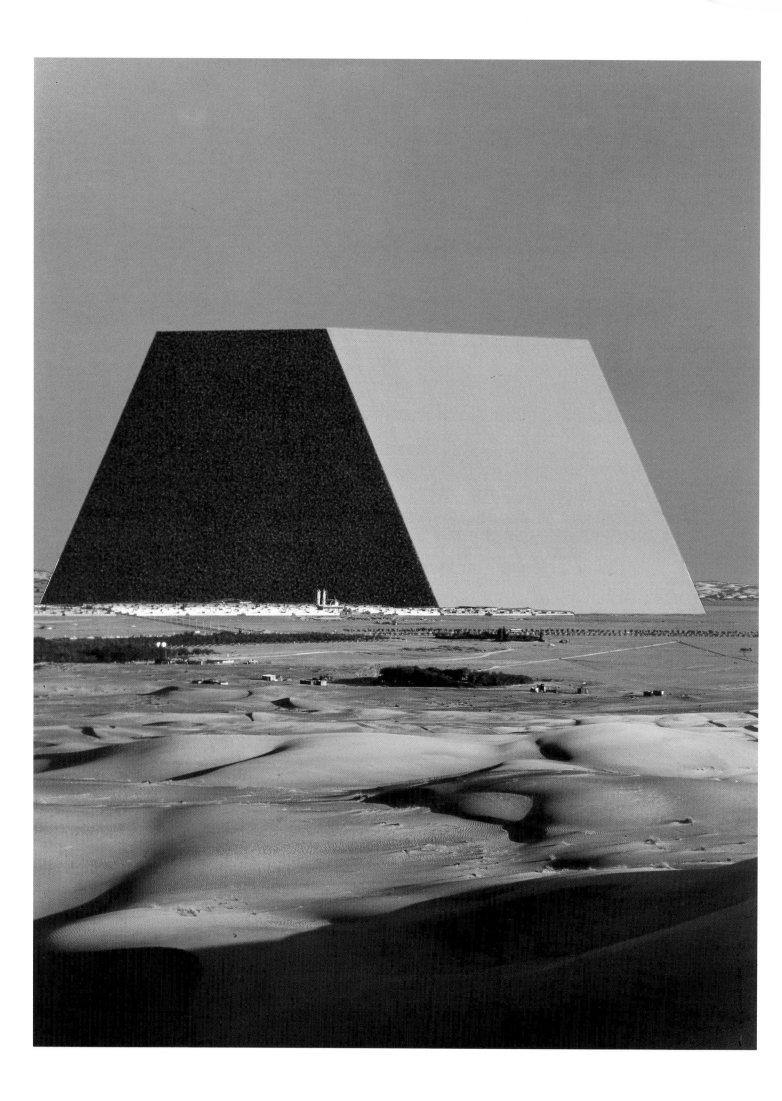

"This is reality"
Work in progress

The Christos are not artists who stand still. In keeping with the emphasis on temporary states, their work is forever moving on from one project to the next; and their works in progress inevitably overlap. Even as the Reichstag project moves towards realization at long last, the Christos are absorbed in other ideas, some of which have occupied them for years. There is something monumental in this ability to conceive art across long time spans.

The principal works by the Christos currently in progress, the Reichstag aside, are *The Mastaba of Abu Dhabi, Project for the United Arab Emirates* (p. 88); *The Gates Project for Central Park New York City* (pp. 90–91); and *Over the River, Project for the Western USA* (pp. 92–93), the exact location of which has not yet been decided at the time of writing.

The *Mastaba* project has a prehistory. A mastaba was an ancient architectural form (a tomb) with two vertical walls, two slant walls, and a flat top. In 1968, the Christos made their first project with this title, consisting of over 1,200 oil barrels, in connection with their exhibition at the Institute of Contemporary Art in Philadelphia. The structure – over 6 meters high, 9 wide, and 12 deep – was installed inside the Museum. Then in 1969 the Christos worked on a mastaba for Houston, Texas, consisting of 124,000 barrels. Christo produced drawings, pastels and collages, but the project was not realized.

The Mastaba of Abu Dhabi is conceived as a symbol of the Emirate and of the greatness of Sheikh Zayed, according to the Christos' release, and of "the civilization of oil throughout the world". It is planned to be higher and more massive than the Pyramid of Cheops near Cairo. There is a self-evident logic, of course, in choosing the world's greatest oil-producing center, the Gulf, as the site for a project that will use almost 400,000 oil barrels. Another logic of a more whimsically appealing nature lies in the proposed accord between oil barrels of many and various colors and Islamic tile mosaics: this level of analogy arguably makes *The Mastaba of Abu Dhabi* one of the Christos' most challenging projects.

A mastaba was originally an ancient Egyptian tomb in which offerings were made in an outer chamber. In an inner chamber would be a figure of the deceased person, with a shaft leading down to the grave proper. In other words, a mastaba had a purpose: sacred, ritual, devotional, it was a monument that served memory and honor. Their projected *Mastaba* is quite unlike this; its sole purpose is to exist, as a large sculptural artefact. The barrels, lain horizontally on their sides, will (if the project is realized) add up to a total structure so large that a number of forty-story skyscrapers could comfortably be fitted into the volume; but there will be no ingress except for a passageway to an elevator to take visitors to the top, 150 meters above ground level, from where they will enjoy views 50 kilometers into the surrounding country. The sense of occasion, the experience of the thing, will be its entire purpose.

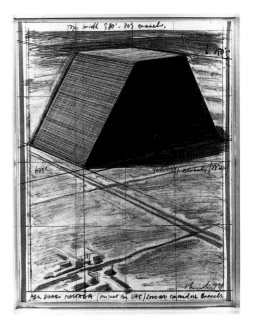

The Mastaba of Abu Dhabi, Project for the United Arab Emirates
Drawing, 1978
Pencil, charcoal, pastel and crayon, 71 x 56 cm
Private collection

PAGE 88:
The Mastaba of Abu Dhabi, Project for the United Arab Emirates (detail)
Collaged photograph, 1979, 56 x 35 cm
New York, Collection Jeanne-Claude Christo

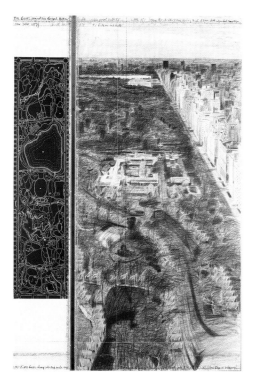

The Gates, Project for Central Park, New York City
Drawing, 1991, in two parts
Pencil, charcoal, pastel, crayon and map
203.6 x 38 and 203.6 x 106.6 cm
New York, Collection Jeanne-Claude Christo

Refusal report by the New York Parks Commissioner on the temporary work of art *The Gates, Project for Central Park, New York City*, 1981

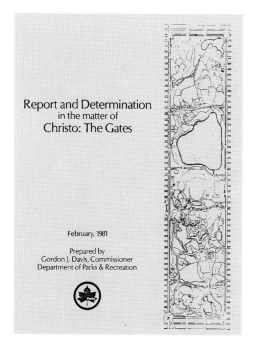

The walkways' area approaching the *Mastaba* will strike the visitor as an oasis, with its flowers and grass. Palm trees, eucalyptus, thorns and other shrubs will also be planted around the mastaba at some distance, to serve as a windbreak, minimizing the force of sandstorms and winds. The project description envisions a "worship room" (as well as parking and other facilities) in this somewhat distant area; the mention of worship is a tactful reminder of the original function of such structures, and a courtesy to the Islamic world, but at present, despite the Christos' having published a detailed exhibition catalogue in Arabic, the project has not been approved.

The Gates, Project for Central Park, New York City represents a lighter side of the Christos' work, the side seen so well in *The Umbrellas* or *Surrounded Islands*, rather than the monumental side that has repeatedly been drawn to massive architectural structures. *The Gates* are planned to be about five meters high, the width varying to suit the width of the paths, and will be set up on the pathways of Central Park, spaced at intervals of about three meters. Attached to the top of each steel frame will be an orange-colored fabric panel; in the right breeze, these synthetic woven panels will wave aloft towards the next gate.

When the Christos originally conceived the project in 1980, they hoped that installation could be effected for a fortnight in October 1983 or 1984; but in fact the project has yet to be realized. At the time, they provided written undertakings that neither New York City nor the park would bear any of the expenses, and proposed drawing up a contract similar to that made with the authorities in California for the *Running Fence* project. Such a contract would require the Christos to provide personal and property insurance exempting the Department of Parks from all liability; to prepare a statement on the project's environmental impact, if required; to restore all the park territory involved to its original state after the removal of *The Gates*; and, throughout, to co-operate fully with all the relevant authorities. The Christos proposed to employ only Manhattan residents for the work, to pay the cost of Park supervision, and to guarantee access for maintenance and all emergency vehicles. They also assured that no rock or vegetation formations would be disturbed, or wildlife patterns interfered with. In a word, the Christos made their proposal in a manner that has become tantamount to a trademark: well thought out, scrupulous, considerate, diplomatic, and, above all, with an attractive sense of organized responsibility. The tactics have become part of the art.

The Gates project would underline the organic, in an airy contrast with the geometrical grid of Manhattan. It would complement the beauty of Central Park. At present, though, the project remains unrealized. In the 1980s, after the Christos had submitted detailed proposals and studies, the City Commissioner of Parks unfortunately issued a 200-page report refusing permission.

Over the River (pp. 92–93), the Christos' newest project, was begun in 1992. Christo made drawings and collages of several potential sites (but at the time of writing no decision on a location has yet been taken, nor on the color of fabric to be used). The concept involves suspending fabric panels horizontally above the waters of a river, following its shapes and course and changing widths where the waters are calm, and equally where they are white with turbulence. Steel cables anchored on the banks will serve to hang woven nylon panels, down to within 4–8 meters of the water, and these draped panels will be arranged along a length of river 6.5 to 10 kilometers long, with interruptions for bridges, rocks, trees or bushes allowing light to flow in copiously. Covered or tented, the river will be transformed by the luminous play of sunlight through the fabric, and for two weeks *Over the*

The Gates, Project for Central Park, New York City
Collage, 1994 in two parts
Pencil, fabric, charcoal, crayon and map
30.5 x 77.5 and 66.7 x 77.5cm
New York, Collection Jeanne-Claude Christo

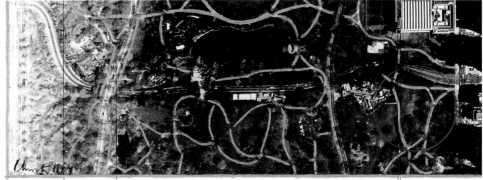

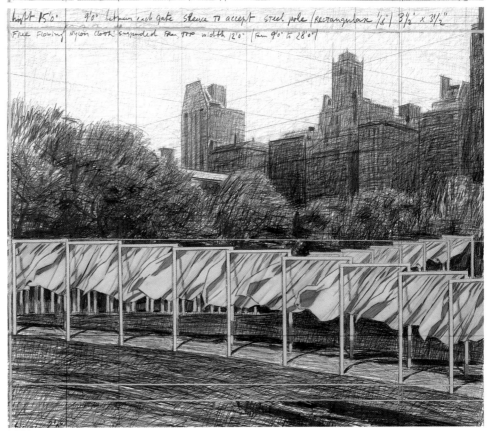

River, all being well, will be a rare and unusual enhancement of the natural and recreational river environment.

Christo's limited editions of lithographs, prints and objects (of which some 150 have appeared since 1963) contain work of extraordinary value – and have served a variety of purposes essential to the Christos' more familiar and spectacular projects. Sales of these editions raise funds; and financing costly public projects is always a challenge. (Even so, the Christos have made numerous goodwill donations to museums and institutions.) The editions constitute records of projects realized or not, and are thus an invaluably permanent archive of the Christos' temporary art.

The first of Christo's editions (in 1963) was the folded and wrapped German weekly news magazine *Der Spiegel* (p.26) (each object in the edition containing a different issue). It was followed by a wrapped *Look* magazine, roses, and boxes. There were editions related to the *Store Fronts* or the Kassel *Air Package* (1968, p.35), to projects for a wrapped Arc de Triomphe or the National Gallery of Modern Art in Rome, the wrapped Australian coastline and the *Valley Curtain* (p.40), and many more, in a variety of forms: as lithographs, collages, scale models, and as limited editions of photographs by

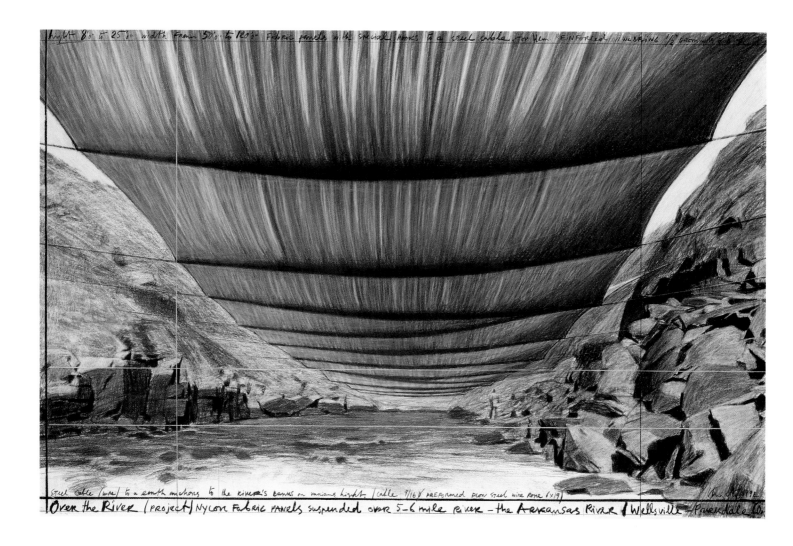

Over the River, Project for the Arkansas River, Colorado
Drawing, 1992
Pencil, charcoal, pastel and crayon,
106.6 x 165 cm
New York, Collection Jeanne-Claude Christo

Harry Shunk and Wolfgang Volz. Christo's work in this field is too diverse and prolific to give any full account of it here, but the reader can be referred to the excellent catalogue raisonné published in 1988 by Edition Schellmann (Munich/New York), an updated edition of which is cur-rently in preparation. In addition, the gifted Wolfgang Volz, long-time friend and associate of the Christos, has produced portfolios of photographs of the *Running Fence*, *Surrounded Islands* and other projects. By all of these means an art essentially temporary is enabled to make an enduring impact, not only in the memories of those who witnessed the Christos' creations on site.

In a working life in art that now spans over three decades, the Christos have created a vast and diverse body of work, and, while never ceasing to attract controversy, now number not only among the best known but also (a rare gift) among the most loved and respected of contemporary artists. The global scope of their artistic thinking is apparent both in their striking choices of locations and in their undauntedness in the face of difficulties. Global scope too often implies commercial trivialization, but the Christos are quick to make the necessary distinctions. "Most art," Christo has observed, "comes in the form of blockbuster exhibitions, which are little better than Disneyland. Our projects are once-in-a-lifetime experiences. They are about freedom. Our bourgeois society has the notion of art as merchandise available only to limited audiences. With our art you do not need tickets to see it." In this antipathy to conventional ideas of art consumption, we can detect both Christo's roots in the Communist bloc and an entirely individual determination to serve populist ideals of universal availability. At the same time, the unfailing energy, vision and commitment of both Christo and

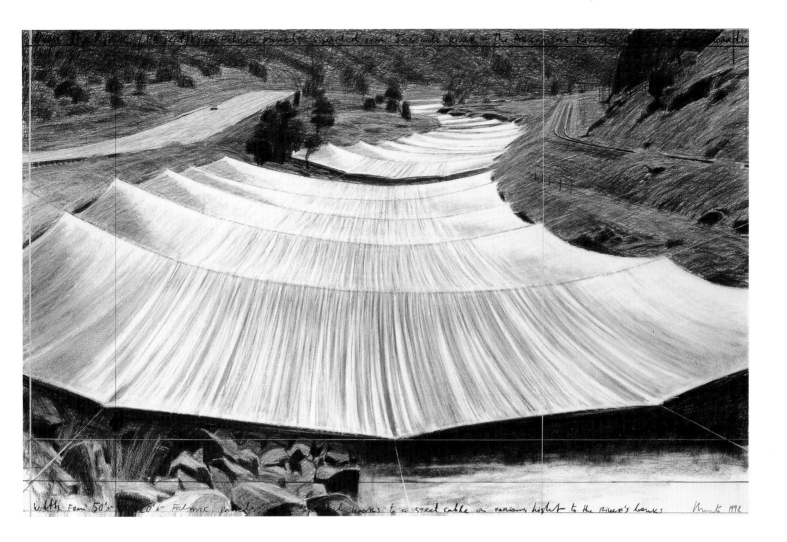

Over the River, Project for the Arkansas River, Colorado
Drawing, 1992
Pencil, charcoal and pastel crayon,
106.6 x 165 cm
New York, Collection Jeanne-Claude Christo

Jeanne-Claude have equipped them perfectly for success in an art world in-creasingly governed by market forces, a world that now requires artists to have unusual drive.

Speaking about their philosophy behind their projects, Christo told us: "While our temporary works of art all contain, at various degrees, elements of social, political, economic and environmental concerns, they also have as-pects of painting, architecture, sculpture and urban planning. For instance, the *Surrounded Island* might look like a giant flat shaped canvas. *The Pont Neuf Wrapped* with its folds and draperies shows the image of a classical sculpture, but the bridge, while wrapped continued to be architecture, people were walking on the bridge, cars were rolling, boats were passing under the arches. *The Umbrellas, Japan–USA* definitely had more to do with urban planning, it included the rice fields, gas stations, houses, grazing land, chur-ches, temples, schools, hills, river, mountains.

When we are asked by painters or sculptors how we can work for 4 or 6 or 10 or 21 years on the same project, they do not realize what is inherent to each one of our works, they would not ask the same question to architects or urban planners, because it is obvious that creating a bridge, a skyscraper, a highway or an airport does take many years."

I shall give Christo himself the last word. Interviewed by *Balkan Maga-zine* (November/December 1993) he remarked: "Our projects are not some-thing out of fantasy. Fantasy is what we find in the cinema and the theatre, our imaginative notion of things. But when we feel the real wind, the real sun, the real river, the mountain, the roads – this is reality, and we use it in our work. Our projects carry that reality."

Christo and Jeanne-Claude – Chronology

1935 Christo: born Christo Javacheff, June 13, Gabrovo, of an Bulgarian industrialist family.
Jeanne-Claude: born Jeanne-Claude de Guille-bon, June 13, Casablanca, of a French military family.

1952 Jeanne-Claude: Baccalauréat in Latin and Philosophy, University of Tunis.

1953 Christo: studies at Fine Arts Academy, Sofia.

1956 Christo: arrival in Prague.

1957 Christo: one semester's study at the Vienna Fine Arts Academy.

1958 Christo: arrival in Paris where he meets Jeanne-Claude. *Packages* and *Wrapped Objects*.

1960 Birth of their son, Cyril, May 11.

1961 Project for a *Wrapped Public Building*. *Stacked Oil Barrels* and *Dockside Packages, Cologne Harbor*.

1962 *Wall of Oil Barrels – Iron Curtain* blocking the Rue Visconti, Paris. *Stacked Oil Barrels* in Gentilly, near Paris. *Wrapping a Girl*, London.

1963 *Showcases*.

1964 Establishment of permanent residence in New York City. *Store Fronts*.

1966 *Air Package* and *Wrapped Tree*, Stedelijk van Abbe Museum, Eindhoven. *1,200 Cubic Meter Package*, Walker Art Center, Minneapolis School of Art.

1968 *Wrapped Fountain* and *Wrapped Medieval Tower*, Spoleto. Wrapping of a public building, *Kunsthalle Berne*. *5,600 Cubic Meter Package*, documenta IV, Kassel, an Air Package 85 meters high, 10 meters in diameter. *Corridor Store Front*, total area: 139 square meters. *1,240 Oil Barrels Mastaba*, and *Two Tons of Stacked Hay*, Philadelphia Institute of Contemporary Art.

1969 *Museum of Contemporary Art, Chicago, Wrapped*. *Wrapped Floor and Stairway*. 260 square meter drop cloths, Museum of Contemporary Art, Chicago. *Wrapped Coast, Little Bay, Australia,* 92,900 square meters, erosion-control fabric and 56 kilometers of ropes. Project for Stacked Oil Barrels, *Houston Mastaba, Texas*. 1,249,000 barrels. Project for *Closed Highway*.

1970 *Wrapped Monument to Vittorio Emanuele, Piazza del Duomo, Milan,* and *Wrapped Monument to Leonardo da Vinci, Piazza della Scala, Milan*.

Jeanne-Claude and Christo in Kansas City, 1978

Christo and Jeanne-Claude in Miami, 1983

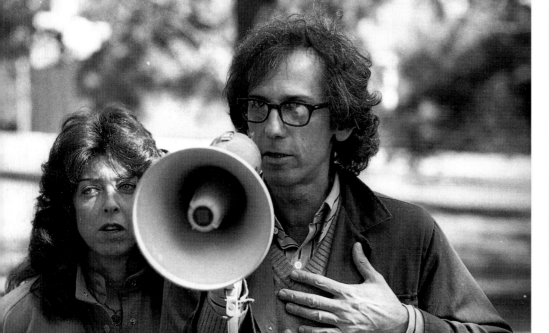

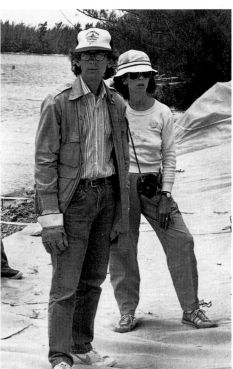

Christo in his studio, 1988

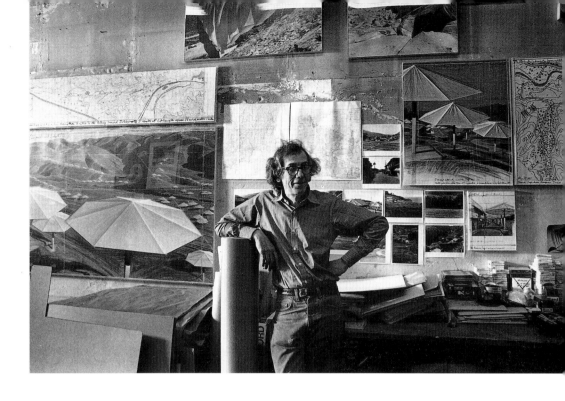

1971 *Wrapped Floors and Covered Windows,* Museum Haus Lange, Krefeld, West Germany.

1972 Start of *Wrapped Reichstag, Project for Berlin.*
Valley Curtain, Rifle, Colorado, 1970–1972. Width: 381 meters, height: 111 meters.

1974 *The Wall, Wrapped Roman Wall, Via Veneto and Villa Borghese, Rome.*
Ocean Front, Newport, Rhode Island. 14,000 square meters of floating polypropylene fabric over the ocean.

1976 *Running Fence, Sonoma and Marin Counties, California, 1972–1976,* 5.5 m high, 39.5 km long, 200,000 square meters of woven nylon fabric, 145 km of steel cables, 2,060 steel poles (each: 9 cm in diameter, 6.4 meters long).

1978 *Wrapped Walk Ways, Jacob L. Loose Park, Kansas City, Missouri, 1977–1978,* 12,540 square meters of woven nylon fabric over 4.5 km of walkways.

1979 *The Mastaba of Abu Dhabi, Project for the United Arab Emirates* (in progress).

1980 *The Gates, Project for Central Park, New York City* (in progress).

1983 *Surrounded Islands, Biscayne Bay, Greater Miami, Florida, 1980–1983,* 603,850 square meters of pink woven polypropylene fabric.

1984 *Wrapped Floors and Stairways* of Architecture Museum, Basle, Switzerland.

1985 *The Pont Neuf Wrapped, Paris, 1975–1985,* 40,876 square meters of woven polyamide fabric. 13 kilometers of rope.

1991 *The Umbrellas, Japan – USA 1984–1991,* 1,340 blue umbrellas in Ibaraki, Japan; 1,760 yellow umbrellas in California, USA. Height: 6 meters, diameter: 8.66 meters.

1992 *Over The River, Project for Western USA* (in progress).

1995 *Wrapped Floors and Stairways and covered Windows,* Museum Würth, Künzelsau, Germany.
Wrapped Reichstag Berlin, 1971–1995.

Christo and General Jacques de Guillebon, Jeanne-Claudes father, 1976

In front of The Pont Neuf Wrapped, 1985

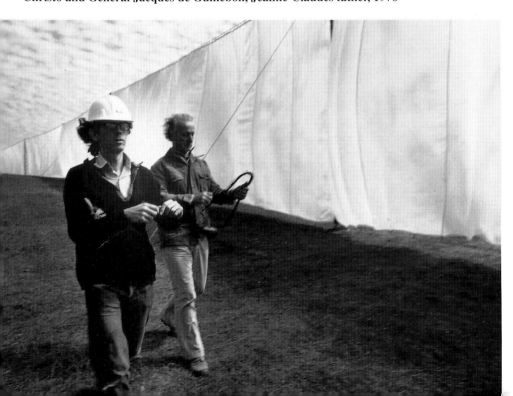

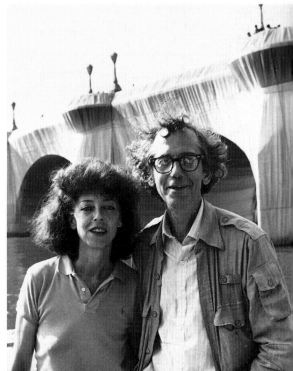

In this series:

- Arcimboldo
- Bosch
- Botticelli
- Bruegel
- Cézanne
- Chagall
- Christo
- Dalí
- Degas
- Delaunay
- Duchamp
- Ernst
- Gauguin
- van Gogh
- Grosz
- Hopper
- Kahlo
- Kandinsky
- Klee
- Klein
- Klimt
- Lempicka

- Lichtenstein
- Macke
- Magritte
- Marc
- Matisse
- Miró
- Monet
- Mondrian
- Munch
- O'Keeffe
- Picasso
- Rembrandt
- Renoir
- Rousseau
- Schiele
- von Stuck
- Toulouse-Lautrec
- Turner
- Vermeer
- Warhol

The publisher wishes to thank Christo, Jeanne-Claude and Wolfgang Volz for their kind premission to reproduce the illustrations and for their support and encouragement in the preparation of this book. In addition to the collections and institutions named in the captions, the following acknowledgements are also due to the photographers:

Klaus Baum: 35
Ferdinand Boesch: 30
Simon Chaput: 92, 93

Jeanne-Claude Christo: 36, 52, 61, 63, 95
Thomas Cugini: 37
Michael Cullen: 80, 84, 85, 87
Deutsche Luftbild: 84
Hans-Peter Dimke: 86
Eeva-Inkeri: 12, 13, 14, 15, 18, 25, 26, 27, 30, 50, 61, 80, 81
Gianfranco Gorgoni: 48, 50
André Grossmann: 9, 51, 90
Carroll T. Hartwell: 33
Jean-Dominique Lajoux: 16
Raymond de Seynes: 31

Harry Shunk: 20, 21, 23, 25, 32, 34, 37, 38, 39, 40, 41, 42, 43, 44, 45, 47, 48, 49
Wolfgang Volz: 1, 2, 6, 7, 8 (Aleks Percovic), 9 (Aleks Percovic), 10, 11, 19, 24, 25, 28, 51, 53, 54, 55, 56, 57, 58, 59, 60, 62, 64, 65, 66, 67, 68, 69, 70, 71, 72, 73, 74, 75, 76, 77, 78, 79, 82, 83, 85, 88, 89, 90, 91, 94, 95
John Webb: 23
Stephan Wewerka: 22
Dimiter Zagoroff: 46